Richard Webster

Principles of Monetary Legislation

With Definite Proposals for Placing the Sound and Successful Principle into

Permanent Operation

Richard Webster

Principles of Monetary Legislation
With Definite Proposals for Placing the Sound and Successful Principle into Permanent Operation

ISBN/EAN: 9783744720205

Printed in Europe, USA, Canada, Australia, Japan

Cover: Foto ©Suzi / pixelio.de

More available books at **www.hansebooks.com**

PRINCIPLES

OF

MONETARY LEGISLATION

WITH

DEFINITE PROPOSALS FOR PLACING THE SOUND

AND SUCCESSFUL PRINCIPLE INTO

PERMANENT OPERATION

BY

RICHARD WEBSTER

LONDON

LONGMANS, GREEN, AND CO.

1874

.

TO

HUGH MASON, ESQ.

PRESIDENT

FOR THREE SUCCESSIVE YEARS

OF

THE MANCHESTER CHAMBER OF COMMERCE

THIS WORK IS

𝕽espectfully Inscribed

BY

THE AUTHOR

CONTENTS.

CHAPTER III.

PROPOSED PRINCIPLE OF MONETARY LEGISLATION, AND DEFINITE SUGGESTIONS FOR PLACING IT INTO OPERATION.

CHAPTER IV.

OVER-ISSUES, SPECULATION, &c.

PRINCIPLES

OF

MONETARY LEGISLATION.

INTRODUCTION.

No BRANCH OF POLITICAL ECONOMY has received more general attention than the monetary section, and yet, in no other branch, has less real progress been made. Whilst the improvement of the financial machinery has kept pace with the ever-increasing strain thrown upon it by the rapid increase in exchange operations and with the growth of the enormous masses of wealth to be manipulated, the science itself has undergone no corresponding advance, and is still in its infancy. The world has not yet emerged out of the panic period of finance— a period strewn with terrible disasters in the past, and fraught with ever-increasing danger to the future.

The universal application of the principle of division of labour, not only as between individuals and sections in the same country, but as between

B

nations occupying different portions of the face of the globe, renders it a matter of the greatest concern that a determined effort be made to place on a safe and secure basis the vast system of exchanges which arises out of this principle. The division having now reached a higher stage of development than at any prior period—each nation applying itself to a greater extent to those branches of production to which the soil, climate, position, or genius of its people is most peculiarly adapted, with the view to exchanging the surplus for the products of other countries, international commerce is assuming vast dimensions;—the mutual dependence of nations upon one another is becoming deeper; and it is an object worthy of the highest statesmanship to aim at placing on a sound and solid basis, the financial arrangements by which these exchanges are conducted. In no other country has, what may be termed, the international division of labour, been pushed to a greater extent than in this. Whether for good or for evil, we are rapidly transforming 'Merrie England' into the huge workshop of the world, and are year by year becoming more dependent upon other countries for the food supply of our people. We are building up a social fabric such as the world has never before seen—a fabric resting upon our ability to command the first necessaries of life by the exchange of the products of our mines and manufactories for the products of distant climes: and when we pause to reflect upon the fact, that this vast system of production and exchange could not possibly be conducted without the intervention of the financial machinery, we at once perceive the importance of the subject under consideration. Every step in the division of labour beyond what would have been possible under a state of pure barter, rests upon the arrangements by which that boundary line is left in the distance ; and the further we advance from the barter stage, the more complicated and important those arrangements become.

The general object of monetary legislation should be to place these financial arrangements upon just, sound, and secure foundations. The particular object at the present moment should be to put an end to the era of those disasters known as commercial panics. It is high time that monetary science emerged out of the region of neglected truths into its rightful place amongst the useful and applied sciences; and that the crotchets and crude theories of the doctrinaires gave place to sound and comprehensive principles. It is not exclusively with that small section, the currency, that we have to deal, but with the whole of the complicated and important financial arrangements employed in exchange operations, of which banking, in the widest sense of the term, constitutes the centre. The past limitation of the enquiry to the currency section has resulted in the present dead lock on the subject, and it is only by taking a wide and comprehensive view of the matter that any advance can be made.

The subject has been treated in such a narrow and unscientific manner, and with such an utter disregard of the elementary truths of political economy and the rules of strict reasoning and investigation, that at the present moment there is probably no other branch of human enquiry in so deplorable and unsatisfactory a condition. There is no paucity of data out of which to evolve the truths which underlie the subject. The central power of every state has been again and again directed to the accumulation of enormous masses of evidence; the political econo· mists of Europe and America have vied with one another in trying to solve the problem; a perfect host of pamphleteers have inundated the world with their crude theories and panaceas; and yet, the result up to the present moment is, that confusion has been made worse confounded.

This is greatly attributable to the line of attack adopted by the opponents of our present monetary system. That system is founded on definite principles which have been distinctly stated and laid down, and its defence has been conducted with consummate skill by placing those principles in the front rank, to meet every attack, crush every proposal, and generally to defend the position. Instead of boldly grappling with this advanced line, the opponents of the system have vainly endeavoured to carry the position by a series of weak, isolated, and unsupported flank movements, which not only ended in failure but lent a fictitious strength to the line of defence. Stated shortly those principles are : 1. That a pure metallic currency is the perfect type to which a mixed currency of metal and paper should be made to conform in its fluctuations in quantity and value. 2. That a pure metallic currency would fluctuate with the foreign exchanges, and that a mixed currency should therefore be made to do so. This dogma constitutes the centre of the theory on which our present monetary system is based ; and if it is sound, then the disastrous system based upon it is also sound—that system being its logical sequence. Being wrapped up in technical phraseology it has been considered abstruse, but I shall have no difficulty in showing that the reverse is the case, and that it is simply absurd. The main issues are eminently capable of being tested by a number of the best known and most firmly established facts, and those facts afford the most complete and satisfactory refutation to this dogma, and its satellite the system, which the most severe logician could possibly desire to possess.

That a careful reconsideration of the whole matter is required was evidenced by the occurrences of November 1873. The drain of gold to Germany and America trebled the rate of discount here within the short space of six weeks, and had it proceeded to the extent of a few millions more, our financial machinery would have been completely deranged and paralyzed, and the country have been plunged into the grave disaster of a panic. That the

industrial, commercial, and vast financial operations
of a country possessing such enormous wealth and
resources as this should at any time depend upon
the possession of some nineteen millions instead of
fifteen or sixteen millions of gold, and that the
withdrawal of three or four millions would absolutely have deranged our financial machinery,
paralyzed the operations of the whole country, and
produced immense misery, loss, and distress, is on
the face of it a very anomalous thing, and affords
presumptive evidence that monetary science is not
in this country in a very satisfactory condition.

Great impatience and deep dissatisfaction exist
at the continuance of the present state of legislation
on the subject. The body commercial is agitating, in
its Chambers of Commerce throughout the country,
for the removal of the central financial danger under
which operations are being conducted, and something must and will be done. It is of the greatest
importance that this something shall be in the right
direction, but unless sound views are established,
it will more probably be a move in the wrong
direction. The proposals made by the late Government, under the pressure brought to bear upon them
in the early part of the session of 1873, afford
a warning which cannot with impunity be neglected.
The measures proposed would have placed the present system into more complete operation, and have
increased the very evils of which we have so long
and loudly complained. It was proposed to vest

in the Chancellor of the Exchequer the power of
suspending the existing restriction on the Bank
of England issues, this power to be, however, only
exercised after all the evils of the system had been
carefully created and largely inflicted. The conditions on which the power was to be exercised were
(1) That the internal circulation should be at the
time rendered ineffective by panic; (2) That the
foreign exchanges should be favourable to this
country; and (3) That the rate of interest charged
by the Bank for loans, should be 12 per cent.
The first condition was bad enough, but the second
and third effectually surpassed it. Under the second
the panic of 1866 would have been allowed to
continue its destructive progress, and under the
second and third combined, the flame of distrust
would have been so fed, that the foreign exchanges
would have grown more and more unfavourable as
long as we owed a sixpence to any creditor abroad.
These extraordinary proposals were received by
the City and the whole country with profound
astonishment, and yet they were in complete conformity with the general principle of monetary
legislation acted upon by us. The imperative
necessity of enquiring into the grounds on which
that principle is founded will therefore be at once
perceived.

CHAPTER I.

PRINCIPLES OF MONETARY LEGISLATION.

§ 1. THERE are two distinct principles of monetary legislation alternately acted upon by this country. One is embodied in the Bank Acts of 1844 and 1845 ; the other has been repeatedly placed into temporary operation for the express purpose of rescuing us from the grave perils to which we were being exposed by the first. They are in every respect the complete converse of each other, the one regulating the currency by the foreign exchanges in utter disregard of all the consequences to our financial arrangements ; the other protecting those arrangements from the foreign exchanges and all other disturbing causes. The one, has repeatedly plunged the country into great disasters,—the other, has invariably rescued us from the danger : and yet, no sooner has it done so than its disastrous rival has been reinstated in its stead. This is a startling and remarkable fact, and one well calculated to arrest attention and challenge investigation. I propose to prove that it is as true as it is startling ; that the disastrous policy is founded on a fallacy ; and that the solution of this great problem will be found to lie in the complete abandonment of the general, and the permanent adoption of the hitherto temporary policy.

The first principle of monetary legislation, viz. that of securing the convertibility of the note by regulating the currency by the foreign exchanges— utterly regardless of the consequences to the rest of our financial machinery and to the interests dependent thereon, has been practically acted upon in this country ever since the latter end of the last century. In 1844–1845 it was, however, embodied in the Bank Acts of those years. The two Acts were intended to place the same principle into mechanical operation, and in order to avoid repetition and confusion, I will therefore adopt the usual course and speak of them as the Act of 1844.

The object of the Act is thus stated by its author :—

I say that the Bill of 1844 had a triple object. Its first object was that in which I admit it has failed, namely, to prevent by early and gradual, severe and sudden contraction, and the panic and confusion inseparable from it; but the Bill had two other objects of at least equal importance. The one to maintain and guarantee the convertibility of the paper into gold, the other to prevent the difficulties which arise at all times from undue speculation being aggravated by the abuse of paper credit in the form of promissory notes. In these two objects my belief is that the Bill has completely succeeded.—*Sir Robert Peel—Debate on Commercial Distress, December* 3, 1847.

In its first object it has not only completely and confessedly failed, but, as I shall eventually show, it has aggravated the very evil which it was intended to prevent.

With respect to its third object, I shall have occasion further on to prove that the extent and importance of the abuse alluded to was very greatly exaggerated, and that in trying to prevent a comparatively small evil, far greater ones are inflicted.

The remaining object of the Act, that of securing the convertibility of the note, was, however, really its principal object, and it must be candidly admitted that in this it has succeeded; but whether the convertibility would have continued intact if the operation of the Act had not been suspended in 1847, 1857, and 1866 is an open question. Its defenders, however, appear to be satisfied that it is well calculated to secure the convertibility, and contend that the degree of success attained, proves that it is based upon sound principles, which only require to be placed into more perfect operation, as Mr. Lowe proposed to do, to work with complete satisfaction. I join issue with them on this point. It is undoubtedly indispensable to a sound monetary system that the convertibility of the note be carefully maintained, but, as I propose to prove, the means at present employed for the attainment of that desirable object are unsound in principle and disastrous in practice.

This principle of regulating the currency by the foreign exchanges was adopted for the purpose of protecting the convertibility of the note from one particular source of danger, or rather supposed source of danger, viz. that supposed to arise from the currency not fluctuating as a purely metallic currency would have done; viz. contract when, the foreign exchanges being against us, gold was flowing out of the country; and expand when, the foreign exchanges being favourable, gold was flowing into this country. A pure metallic currency was regarded as the perfect type to which a mixed currency of metal and paper should be made to conform in its fluctuations in quantity, in order to secure and protect the convertibility of the note.

This is the fundamental dogma on which our monetary legislation is built, and which I propose to controvert and overthrow. It dates from the same period as that mercantile theory of trade which regarded gold as the only desirable form of wealth, and attempted by a system of legislative restrictions and monopolies to secure to this country a constant inflow of gold; and it is high time that it shared the same fate and was exploded and abandoned.

It cannot be too carefully borne in mind that the Act was devised to guard the note against one particular supposed source of danger, viz. the loss of convertibility, arising from the non-fluctuation of the currency with the foreign exchanges resulting in the complete exhaustion of our stock of gold. The disregard of this important point has led to a very large amount of confusion on the part of the opponents of the system, and the controversy has con-

sequently been fought on false issues. The futility
of showing that the Act is attended with evil consequences is apparent when we remember that those
evils are represented as being inevitable. What requires to be done is to prove that they are not inevitable, and that the grounds upon which that opinion
is honestly held, are unsound.

This principle of regulation is thus laid down
by its advocates :—

If we admit the principle of a metallic standard, and
admit that a paper currency ought to be regulated by
immediate reference to the foreign exchange—that there
ought to be early contraction of paper on the efflux of
gold, we might, I think, infer from reasoning, without
the aid of experience, that an unlimited competition in
respect to issue will not afford a security for the proper
regulation of a paper currency.—*Sir Robert Peel—Debate
on Bank Charter Act, May* 6, 1844.

It is important that a paper currency should be made
to conform to what a metallic currency would be, and
especially that it should be kept at the same value with
the metallic currency by being kept at all times of the
same amount. Now the influx of gold is the only sure
test of what would have been the variations of a metallic
currency, and therefore I conceive that that constitutes
the only proper rule by which to regulate the fluctuations
of a paper currency.—*Commons' Report,* 1840–41—*Lord
Overstone's Evidence,* 2654.

1548.—Does not that state of things (all the exchanges, with the exception of the American, being
favourable, and this exception being caused by the great
import of corn, and ceasing to be of any importance after
the month of April) show that this pressure, admitted to
be distressing to trade, was not necessary, as you suppose

it to have been, for the purpose of correcting adverse exchanges?—I am not able to state whether the facts enumerated in the early part of the question are correct or not, but I am willing to assume that they are correctly stated; but that assumption does not in any degree, in my judgment, invalidate the reasonings by which my previous answers have been guided. I apprehend that the influx or efflux of bullion is the simple fact by which the amount of the circulation ought to be regulated, without reference to the consideration of the quarters, more or less in number, to which the drain goes. If the circulation was a metallic circulation, the drain would, though it proceed to the United States, reduce, *pro tanto*, the metallic money of the country, regulated upon a metallic basis. Why, it may be asked, does gold upon the balance go out of the country? No rational or scientific answer can be given to that question except this, viz., that such is the state of the circulation of the country, as compared with the circulation of other countries, that gold is a cheaper commodity for export than other commodities. So long as that is the fact it is necessary that a contraction of the currency should take place for the purpose of reducing international trade to its only legitimate normal condition, a trade of barter.—*Lord Overstone's Evidence*, 1848.

[The real cause of this drain was stated in the question, but Lord Overstone preferred theory to fact. The rational, scientific, and true answer was that the drain was caused, not by an excess of currency, but by the extra importation of corn consequent upon the deficiency in the harvest and the failure of the Irish potato crop. The exportation of our goods to America not increasing to a corresponding extent, the balance of exchange turned against us, and had to be liquidated in bullion. It was therefore quite unnecessary, on the grounds assigned, to reduce trade to the alarming condition of a trade of barter, a condition under which this country could not support one tenth of its present population.]

[This answer was not, however, much more remarkable than that given to question 1550.]

Are you aware that in April there was the largest export of gold to the United States of any month in that year?—I do not know, I do not at all know where the gold goes to. If it goes, that is all I ever attend to.— *Lord Overstone's Evidence, Parliamentary Committee,* 1848.

[This kind of *scientific* enquiry fully accounts for the deplorable errors which we are about to examine.]

§ 2. This principle of regulating the currency by the foreign exchanges is founded on the utterly erroneous assumptions: 1. That all drains of gold are caused by a depreciation in our currency, and that the mere fact that gold is being exported is conclusive proof that our currency is depreciated: 2. That the only security for the stoppage of drains consists in the forcible contraction of our currency as they proceed; and that unless this be done, the drains will continue until our bullion reserves are completely exhausted, and the convertibility of the note is lost.

This is the one particular danger against which the system is intended to protect the convertibility of the note, and I propose to demonstrate and place it beyond all doubt or question, that it is purely fictitious and exists in theory only, and not in fact.

These extraordinary assumptions are thus laid down :—

In reference to Thornton's statement of the fact that a very unfavourable balance of trade may be produced by a bad harvest, and consequent importation of food ; and that the demand of foreigners for our goods not increasing in the same ratio, the balance has to be liquidated in bullion, Ricardo contends, ' If we consent to give coin in exchange for goods, it must be from choice, not necessity. We should not *import more goods than we export, unless we had a redundancy of currency*, which it therefore suits us to make part of our exports. The exportation of coin is caused by its *cheapness*, and is not the effect but the cause of an unfavourable balance ; we should not export it if we did not send it to a better market, or if we had any commodity which we could export more profitably. It is a salutary remedy for a redundant currency ; and, as I have already endeavoured to prove that redundancy or excess is only a relative term, it follows that the demand for it abroad arises only from the comparative deficiency of the currency of the importing country, which there causes its superior value.'—*Ricardo's Political Works*, pp. 267–8.

[It will be observed that this is on a par with the preceding evidence of Lord Overstone. As a matter of fact, individuals and nations are frequently compelled to give coin in exchange for goods, not from choice, as here stated, but from necessity, as in 1847 ; and when coin is given in exchange for goods, it is not on account of any difference in its value between individuals, whether in the same or in different countries, but because it is used as a

medium of exchange, both nationally and internationally, and passes from hand to hand, and nation
to nation, as money. As a matter of fact, the exportation of coin is *not* caused by its cheapness, and
is not the cause of an unfavourable exchange, but
the effect. Mr. Ricardo inverted the facts, and the
theory, in the authorship of which he holds a conspicuous place, is the result, is the product, of this
extraordinary and almost incredible inversion of
plain facts.]

Thus specie will be sent abroad to discharge a debt
only when it is superabundant; only when it is the
cheapest exportable commodity.—*Ricardo*, p. 269.

The fact that the exchange has fallen, and that the
bullion is being exported, proves incontrovertibly that it
is redundant; and that, consequently, the Directors of the
Bank of England should immediately set about contracting their issues, to prevent the exhaustion of their coffers.
—*M'Culloch's Notes on ' Wealth of Nations,'* p. 494.

And besides being the natural and proper, these were
in fact the only means by which the value of bullion could
be raised in this country, its demand for foreign remittance checked, and the exchange turned in our favour.—
Vide p. 507.

The fact of the exchange being depressed, and of gold
continuing, for any considerable period, to be demanded
from the Bank and exported, is, independently of all other
considerations, a conclusive proof that the currency is
redundant or depreciated, as compared with the currency
of other countries.— *Vide* p. 493.

Money is exported from the country in preference to
other commodities only because money is in excess, and is
therefore cheaper here than in other countries. But this
excess of quantity is soon corrected, and the money of this
country restored to an equality of value with the money of

other countries by the export of gold, provided the place of the gold thus exported be not supplied by new issues of paper money. But if paper be not contracted on this principle, the security for the certain stoppage of the drain is lost.—*Lord Overstone's Evidence*, 1857, p. 15.

When an adverse exchange has set in, the drain cannot be arrested, nor a due amount of treasure retained by the Bank, until a temporary pressure on the money market shall have so acted, first, on the value of money, and, if necessary, on the price of commodities, as to cause our exports first to equal, then to exceed our imports. The temporary pressure on the money market is not only a necessary consequence of an adverse exchange, but the necessary process through which the adverse exchange can be turned, and the convertibility of the note secured, on which account it is necessary that the power of giving temporary aid, if called for by the mercantile body, at such periods of emergency, should *not* exist.—*Lord Overstone's Reply to London Merchants' Petition*, 1847. *Tracts*, 291.

The foregoing quotations will fully serve the purpose for which they are given, that of clearly and impartially stating the point under consideration. They are the clearest expression of the assumption which I have met with, for, generally speaking, it is surrounded by a mass of cloudy verbiage which completely obscures it and renders difficult its comprehension and detection. They show that the principle of monetary legislation at present acted upon by this country is founded upon the cardinal proposition, that all drains of bullion arise from one sole cause, a depreciation in our currency.

It will be observed that this assumption is not

c

stated by these authorities in the clear and direct
terms to which I have reduced it. Had this been done,
its unsoundness could scarcely have escaped their attention; it, however, logically and inevitably follows
from the propositions laid down, for, unless it is
true that all drains are caused by a depreciation in
our currency, it cannot possibly be true that the
mere existence of a drain is conclusive proof that
our currency is depreciated. This is the cardinal
and fundamental assumption on which the system
rests, and it constitutes the great and main issue of
the whole question. The system founded upon it
is expressly adapted to it, and is applicable only to
a condition of things in which it would be absolutely
true. It treats all drains in the same manner on this
assumption, that they all arise from the same cause,
a redundancy and depreciation in our currency, and
that a contraction is necessary in order to correct
such depreciation and stop the drain.

§ 3. Now it is pre-eminently a practical question, and one which can be settled with the most complete certainty. Fortunately, also, it can be tested
by recent events, by the late prolonged drain
of 1872 and 1873. Was this drain caused by a
depreciation in our currency or not? Most undoubtedly it was not. It is well known that it arose
out of the payment of the French War indemnity;
the adoption by Germany and the Scandinavian
States of a gold currency; and by the financial dis-

turbance in America. The financial arrangements by which the indemnity was paid, gave to Germany the control of the European money market, and it was so exercised as to extract and accumulate 50,000,000l. in gold within two years. France drew bills upon England against that portion of the French loans which was taken up here, and against the proceeds of foreign securities sent over here for sale. These drafts were handed to Germany, and the value was withdrawn in the shape of gold as the German coinage operations rendered it necessary. Germany also shipped a large quantity of her demonetised silver to the East, purchased with it bills upon this country, and in due course withdrew the proceeds in gold.

The United States took upwards of 2,000,000l. from us in the course of a week or two. They commanded it by drafts upon this country drawn partly against shipments of produce, partly against the balance created by the payment of the Alabama indemnity, and partly against loans contracted here.

These facts were so well known and clearly recognised, that it seems almost superfluous to offer any evidence in their confirmation, but they are of such vital importance to the matter under consideration that they cannot be too firmly established, and I will therefore adduce an authority on the point which will, I think, be received with the greatest respect and confidence.

The 'Times' has invariably opposed crude and

rash attempts to interfere with the important question with which we are dealing, and has consistently contended that until the present system has been shown to be ill-founded, it is to the interest of all parties that it should be firmly adhered to ; and the opponents of the Act of 1844, not having yet clearly shown that the principles upon which that measure is based are unsound, the ' Times ' has all along declined to commit itself to off-hand and loose proposals. That journal has, however, not hesitated on several occasions to raise the flag of suspicion, and to deplore the terrible disasters which have from time to time overwhelmed the country.

How comes it, asks the ' Times,' that the rate of discount has jumped up from 3 to 8 per cent. with such unpleasant speed ? The atmosphere of August and of September was so serene that the change may well disconcert us. . . . There are very few merchants or manufacturers who do not in some measure trade on borrowed capital, and a sudden stringency in the terms of accommodation is a source of peril, whilst an absolute refusal to continue or renew an outstanding loan may be a message of sus- pension. . . . The best answer to the question why the Bank rate has risen from 3 to 8 per cent. is to be found in the consideration of the counter question, why the reserve of the Bank of England fell more than five mil- lions in less than three weeks. Was there any process by which it could have been prevented ? The money has gone in all directions. Some of it has passed to Germany, some to France, a large portion to the United States ; some of it has left the till of the Bank to increase for a time the circulation throughout the United Kingdom. . . . The German Government has continued its process of draining the bullion market for the material of its new coinage.—*Times, November* 4, 1873.

Some money dealers in the United States had invested the sums left in their hands in trans-continental railways and other similar undertakings, and when the depositors wanted to have their money repaid, they could not get it. ALL THE PRESSURE THAT HAS FOLLOWED HERE ORIGINATED THERE. Up to the moment the panic in Wall Street began everything was smooth with us; our trade had not been inflated, our reserves were ample, there was an abundance of money coming in every day ready to satisfy on easy terms the demands for its withdrawal, &c. —*Times, November* 8.

The disquieting element of the money market for many months past has not been removed. It is still asserted that the German Government holds bills on London to the extent of seven millions sterling. . . . If the bills have been drawn and accepted we shall have to meet the demand, even though we do not owe the money. *Germany has probably been the most powerful agent in producing the frequent recurrence of financial embarrassment of late,* and it is to Germany that we must refer whatever degree of apprehension we may feel with respect to the immediate future.—*Times, November* 28.

There is not the remotest trace here of the deplorable assumption on which our monetary legislation rests, and is it not evident that these drains cannot in any sense whatever be said to have been caused by a depreciation in our currency? The actual causes were purely external, and arose out of events with which our currency had not the remotest connection; and yet the monetary system of this country is based on the assumption that all drains without exception are caused by the one same and sole cause, a depreciation in our currency. The system is expressly intended to counteract that assumed cause, and is adapted for that hypothetical state of things only; and this utterly erroneous assumption is the sole reason why the practical evils created by the system are inflicted upon the country.

Not only, however, are these assumptions utterly erroneous as tested by recent events, but they are absolutely and altogether unsound.

In the first place, drains are produced by various causes. The precious metals are used in settling the balances which arise between different countries, and these balances are determined and affected by numerous causes. Wars, deficient harvests, foreign loans and enterprises, and changes in the extent and direction of foreign trade often produce heavy adverse balances, and render necessary the transmission from one country to another of large quantities of the precious metals. The assumption that the mere existence of a drain is a conclusive proof that it arises from a depreciation in our currency is therefore altogether unfounded, and all the evils created by the system based on that assumption are quite unnecessary and avoidable. In the words of J. S. Mill :

An exportation of the precious metals often arises from no cause affecting currency or credit, but simply from an unusual extension of foreign payments arising either from the state of the markets for commodities, or from some circumstance not commercial. In this class of causes, four, of powerful operation, are included, of each of which the last fifty years of English history afford repeated instances. The first is that of extraordinary foreign expenditure by Government, either political or military, as in the last war, and particularly in the latter years of it. The second is the case of a large exportation of capital for foreign investment: such as the loans and mining operations which partly contributed to the crisis of 1825; and the American speculations which were the principal cause of the crisis of 1839. The third is the failure of crops which supply the raw material of important manufactures: such as the cotton failure in America, which compelled England, in 1847, to incur unusual liabilities for the purchase of that commodity at an advanced price. The fourth is a bad harvest, and a consequent importation of food, of which the years 1846 and 1847 present an example surpassing all antecedent experience.—*Principles of Political Economy*, vol. ii. p. 215.

It results from the whole tenor of the previous arguments, that it is above all essential to remember that fluctuations in the foreign exchanges can arise not only from one cause but *many*, and that till proof is given that actually another influence is at work than the one which may be selected as possible and plausible, no trustworthy opinion can be formed. It is an error often committed, when scientific subjects are superficially or popularly treated, to consider it enough to point out one cause as sufficiently accounting for any phenomena, regardless of the fact that it is far more important to prove that there was no other cause which could have led to the same results. But on no occasion does this fallacy more frequently blind the judgment than on questions of mercantile finance, possibly because the facts with which they have to deal are so complex and entangled that any clear and intelligible solution of the difficulty is held to be sufficiently satisfactory, without regard to the necessity of applying further tests.—*The Right Hon. G. J. Goschen, Theory of Foreign Exchanges*, p. 89.

Not only, however, are the foreign exchanges affected by every cause which affects the state of international indebtedness, but in this particular country they are affected by a greater number of causes than in any other. England is, in exchange operations, the Clearing-house of the world. In India, China, and various other places bills are drawn upon London, not only against shipments to this country, but also against exports to the United States, Russia, and the Continent generally. And these bills are settled by exchange operations of the most extensive and complicated character, and the folly of our monetary policy is absolutely unbounded. It is founded in complete ignorance of those very facts with which *we* ought to be most conversant.

In the second place, the assumption that unless our currency is contracted as the drains proceed they will continue until our stock of bullion is completely exhausted, is equally false. Drains are absolutely limited in extent, the extent of each depending principally upon the nature of its producing cause. A drain consequent upon a deficiency of the harvest is limited to the extent of the extra expenditure for food, and one consequent upon the negotiation of a foreign loan in our market is limited to the extent of the loan, and so on in other cases. Every drain ceases when its producing causes are exhausted, or when they have been counteracted.

For drains bring into operation counteracting forces. The diminution of our bullion tends to produce a rise in the rate of discount, and to disturb the equilibrium between the rate here and abroad. This causes bills upon this country to be held by the foreign exchange dealers until due, instead of being at once discounted here, and causes money falling due to be left here for temporary employment in the channels of discount, instead of being at once withdrawn. It also attracts capital to this country for investment, and in these various ways tends to arrest the drain. The premium which foreign bills bear in our market at the time when drains are taking place is another powerful correcting force.

Bills are at a premium because a greater money value has been imported than exported, but the premium is itself an extra profit to those who export; besides the price they obtain for their goods, they draw for the amount, and gain the premium. It is, on the other hand, a diminution of profit to those who import. Besides the price of the goods, they have to pay a premium for remittance; so what is called an unfavourable exchange is an encouragement to export, and a discouragement to import; and if the balance due is of small amount, and is the consequence of some merely casual disturbance in the ordinary course of trade, it is soon liquidated in commodities, and the account adjusted by means of bills, without the transmission of bullion.— *J. S. Mill, Principles of Political Economy,* vol. ii. p. 165.

A depreciation of our currency, as compared with the currencies of other countries, means a general rise of prices here, without a corresponding rise abroad. Now if we even admit such a general rise to be possible, still the doctrine would be unsound, for there are other and better remedies for such a state of things than a forcible contraction of the currency, and the reduction of our trade to what Lord Overstone calls ' *its legitimate normal condition, a trade of barter.*'

For even if general prices *were* to be raised by a redundancy in our currency, still they would be corrected in the ordinary course of mercantile dealings. The state of prices in other countries is one of the chief determining causes which regulate prices here, and the falling off or cessation in the demand for our productions, which would inevitably follow such a rise, would lower prices and restore them to a sound and legitimate condition. The assumption that such an artificial rise in prices would continue to exist if we did not forcibly contract our currency as drains proceed, is a complete inversion of the truth ; and not only does it clash with the most elementary laws of value, but it is confuted by daily experience.

The powerful and ever-active laws of supply and demand provide a certain corrective to any such increase in prices. A rise in the price of any great article of exchange, whether arising from an extension of credit in the form of banknotes, or in any other of its various forms ; from speculation fostered by cheap money ; from a combination to ' rig ' any particular market; or from any other cause whatever which is not grounded upon the ordinary laws of supply and demand, cannot but prove to be of a temporary character. The instant the rise has been established forces immediately come into active operation which inevitably draw prices down to their proper level. This is witnessed daily. It is at the present moment correcting the prices of those great articles of exchange, coal and iron. The supply of coal is undergoing such an enormous development on the one hand, and the demand has so fallen off, or become stationary on the other, that a very considerable fall in its price is simply a question of time; and the demand for iron at its present price has so fallen off, as is indicated by the Board of Trade returns, that a fall in the price is inevitable, and must accompany the fall in coal. The absurdity of any proposal to forcibly contract the currency in order to accelerate the restoration of the prices of these two articles to their proper level, at the risk of bringing about a breakdown in our financial machinery and the infliction of immense evils on the whole interests of the country, would be so glaring as to ensure its instant dismissal; and yet that is precisely what we aim at doing by our present monetary system whenever a drain of gold arises. We positively assume that all drains, without exception, arise from a depreciation in our currency, or in other words, from a rise in prices; and we proceed to contract our currency in order to bring about a fall in prices and stop the drain by removing its assumed cause. And it not only aims at doing this altogether unnecessary work, but it blindly enforces the contraction whenever a drain of gold arises, whether the inflation in prices exists or not. It assumes that such inflation does exist whenever gold is flowing out of the Bank, even although that very gold is withdrawn, not for export, but for internal circulation. Anything more outrageously irrational than this was never known.

Values, like the ocean, are governed by opposing forces; some tend to raise, others to lower them, and it would be as rational a proceeding to build a wall to prevent the submersion of the world by the tides, as it is to inflict all the disasters consequent upon the operation of the present monetary system in order to prevent the issue of notes producing a general and artificial rise in prices. Values are constantly oscillating around their mean point, and whether the article is coal, iron, cotton, gold, or anything else, the laws of supply and demand, provided they are not interfered with by monopolies, are in constant operation and may be absolutely depended upon to keep them right in the long run. To legislate to ensure this inevitable result by regulating the currency by the foreign exchanges, is about as rational a proceeding as it would be to aim at doing it by regulating the currency by the barometer.

Had the advocates of the fundamental assumption paused, in their headlong career of error, to consider its logical results, they could not have failed to detect the fraud which their judgment was practising upon their common sense, but instead of doing this, they appear to have resolutely closed their eyes, and to have ceased to be amenable to reason. Strong in their conviction of the absolute soundness of their smooth and delusive theory, they firmly ignored the world of surrounding facts by which it was confuted; or when for a moment they did condescend to deal with facts, they invariably succeeded in interpreting them in their own favour: a species of self-delusion very general and very easy of accomplishment. We have seen that one of these advocates, Lord Overstone, deliberately told the Committee of 1848 that he did not pay any attention to facts. ' I do not know, I do not at all know, where the gold goes to. If it goes, that is all I ever attend to.' According to the theory it went because it was of less value here than abroad, and it therefore appeared to be perfectly immaterial where it went to.

§ 4. The delusion was evidently protected from discovery by the ambiguity of the term ' VALUE.' The important difference between *intrinsic* and *extrinsic* value was lost sight of, and it will assist us in clearing up the matter if we spend a little time in looking into this fallacy of confusion.

The cardinal assumption that all drains of gold are produced by a depreciation in our currency logically and inevitably involves the further assumption that the intrinsic value of gold is constantly fluctuating, for as drains are constantly arising and ceasing, it would logically follow that the depreciation is constantly arising and disappearing; in other words, that the intrinsic value of gold, that is, its exchangeable relation to all other commodities, is constantly fluctuating.

By *intrinsic* value is meant that value of a commodity which depends upon the cost of production &c. of itself; or, in the case of notes and bills of exchange, of the standard of value which those documents represent. Any change in this value alters the exchangeable relations of the article to *all other* things—if it rises, commanding more of all other things, and if it falls, less.

By *extrinsic* value, on the other hand, is meant that value of an article which depends upon the cost of production &c., not of itself, but of other things. Every article has therefore only one intrinsic value, but as many extrinsic values as there are other exchangeable commodities. This distinction is of the greatest importance in the consideration of this matter, and its neglect has led to the fallacy of confusion with which we are dealing.

Now it does not follow because an export of gold arises that its intrinsic value has fluctuated. The fluctuation may have arisen in the value of the bills of exchange, and such is really the case. Bills of exchange constitute one of the extrinsic values of gold, and the reason why gold is exported is because bills have risen in value to that point at which it is cheaper to export gold than to purchase bills for remittance. This one extrinsic value of gold has fallen, but this arises, as the term extrinsic implies, from the intrinsic value of the bills, and not that of the gold having risen. In consequence of an adverse balance of international indebtedness, the demand for bills for remittance exceeds the supply, the payments to be made exceed the payments to be received, and therefore bills, which constitute the ordinary means of remittance, bear a premium, and this premium is added to their price. When the premium rises to that point at which it covers the expense and risk of the remittance of bullion, it is as cheap to remit bullion as to purchase and remit bills, and when it rises above this point, the exportation of bullion becomes a profitable transaction, and the cheapest mode of remittance. Bills can then be created, and gold be remitted in payment of them, at a profit, this consisting of the difference between the premium received on the bills and the cost of transmitting bullion.

That the change is in the *intrinsic* value of the bills, and not in that of the gold, is evident. By *intrinsic* value is meant, as already stated, that value of a commodity which depends upon the cost of production &c. of itself; any change in this value is a change in its relation to all other commodities, in other words, in all its *extrinsic* values.

Now, applying this definition, what do we find? It is found, as a matter of fact, that gold will exchange for precisely the same quantity of all other things, except bills of exchange (all other causes being allowed for), as it would before the drain of gold arose : that prices, or the value of commodities in currency, have not, with this single exception, undergone any fluctuation, which must have been the case if the intrinsic value of gold had varied. The intrinsic value of bills, on the contrary, has fluctuated ; they will command more of all other commodities—all their extrinsic values have changed. The bills will exchange for more money, and a given quantity of money continuing to exchange for the same quantity of other commodities, the increased quantity of money purchased by the bills will purchase an increased quantity of general commodities, therefore *the bills* will purchase an increased quantity of general commodities. It is partly necessary to express the proposition in this syllogistic form, on account of changes in value being commonly expressed in currency. The proposition may be stated in other, and perhaps clearer, terms. Bills have risen in value in relation to all other commodities, they will purchase more gold, corn, iron, coal, &c., and this affords complete evidence that the change has arisen in the intrinsic value of the bills, and not in that of the gold.

This is so very evident that it only requires to be stated to be at once admitted, and yet our monetary system is based on the assumption that it is the intrinsic value of the gold and not of the bills which has fluctuated whenever a drain of bullion arises; and, as we have seen, this error was tenaciously adhered to by Mr. Ricardo and Lord Overstone in the face of undisputed facts which completely demonstrated its unsoundness.

It may be as well to point out that the value of the bills of exchange which enters into the point under consideration is not the nominal value expressed on the face of the bills, but the value which the foreign exchange dealers will give for them. When there is an active enquiry for bills, they will give more than the nominal value for them; when a weak enquiry, less; the amount given being technically termed the current rate of exchange. In other words, they will in the one case pay a premium for the bills, in the other deduct a discount, and it is when the former reaches a certain point that gold begins to flow out; flowing, not on account of any change in its intrinsic value, but as international currency, in liquidation of an adverse balance of international indebtedness.

This point is unavoidably more or less technical, but it would be quite out of place for me to attempt to explain the whole subject of the foreign exchanges. That has been most ably done by Mr. Goschen, to whose work on the 'Theory of the Foreign Exchanges' I am much indebted, and to

D

which I beg to refer those who desire to completely master this branch of the subject.

This fallacy has also been fostered by the ambiguity of the phrase *value of money*. The *loanable* value of money has been confounded with the *intrinsic* value of money, and changes in the rate of discount, which constitute changes in the loanable value, have been treated as synonymous with changes in its intrinsic and exchangeable value. Need I point out that the terms are entirely different, and that while the former value of money is constantly fluctuating, the latter seldom does so. The *intrinsic* value of gold is subject to less variation than that of any other known article, and gold is, for that very reason, so peculiarly adapted to act as a standard of value. And yet the monetary system of this great country is based on the extraordinary assumption that the intrinsic value of gold is constantly fluctuating. As has just been pointed out, this assumption is involved in, and flows from, the cardinal assumption that all drains arise from a depreciation of our currency; for as drains are constantly arising and ceasing, it would follow that the depreciation is constantly arising and disappearing, or, in other words, that the intrinsic value of money is constantly fluctuating.

§ 5. As a matter of fact, gold is employed as international currency in the settlement of international indebtedness, the foreign exchange dealers conducting the settlement and undertaking the export and import of gold and silver whenever large balances arise. Gold is also used as an article of consumption in the arts, and in the manufacture of plate &c., and it flows from country to country on two distinct principles; in the first as an ordinary commodity, in the second as currency. The consumption of the metal in various branches of manufacture is very great, but the demand may, in the absence of any data on the point, be assumed to be steady, and we may also safely assume that the supply and demand is in a state of equilibrium; that is, that trade is so adjusted, that the quantity of gold required for this purpose, is distributed in the same manner as all other commodities.

As currency, it flows between different countries on precisely the same principle as it flows between individuals in the same country; in fact, it is flowing between individuals in both cases. From a commercial point of view, the world is a great mart, in which the various products of different climes are exchanged, and in which gold constitutes a part of the currency. The existence of monopolies, restrictions, &c., on the trade between nations, has led to the opinion that exchanges are conducted on a different principle between nations than between individuals, but this is not true. Restrictions, monopolies, &c., exist at home, and to a great extent necessarily so, but no one for a moment thinks of saying that these alter the principle on which exchanges are conducted. The method, or the extent, may be altered by the existence of these things, but the principle is the same. Gold is, both nationally and internationally, employed as a medium of exchange, in addition to the other purposes to which it is directed. As currency, it is not dealt in · for consumption—as a staple of trade—as the ultimate satisfaction of an exertion—but simply as a medium of exchange. The international currency consists of bills of exchange and the precious metals, but the latter are only employed when there exists a scarcity of the former.

The flows of gold which take place as international currency may be divided into two classes : first, the ordinary, and second, the extraordinary.

By ordinary flows, I mean those which arise in the ordinary course of trade. For instance, a stream of gold is constantly flowing through this country, coming from gold-producing countries, and going to other parts of the world, and as we possess the trade of Australia, the stream is very great. We treat it as currency, receiving it in payment for a portion of our exports, and paying it away in the purchase of a portion of our imports. Australia treats it as a product, in the same manner as we treat our iron ; and the countries to which we pay it away treat it, to a great extent, as an ordinary import for consumption. These two parties are at each end of the stream, and our trade is the channel through which it flows ; but the motive for which they use it, does not affect its relation to ourselves. To us it is a medium of exchange, and we employ gold for this purpose in our foreign trade to a greater extent than any other nation. The imports of gold and silver in 1873 amounted to nearly 34,000,000*l*., and the exports to more than 29,000,000*l*..

By extraordinary flows, I mean those which are produced by extraordinary causes. Such, for instance, as those arising from foreign loans and enterprises; great imports of food, in consequence of deficient harvests; sudden increases in the imports of the raw material of our manufactures, in consequence of political disturbances abroad, and numerous other causes of a similar nature.

Flows of this class produce fluctuations in our stock of bullion to a considerable extent, and it is against these we ought to provide an available fund. Our present system takes the opposite course, attempts to prevent the fund from being used, and disorganises commerce, at the expense of the mercantile and labouring classes, in order to counteract a wild supposition—a false assumption!

It is quite true that gold is not remitted in payment of our indebtedness to other countries so long as the dealers are able to buy a corresponding amount of bills on those countries, but this is simply equivalent to saying that gold is only remitted when balances arise, that is, when the payments to be made are in excess of the payments to be received. When this is the case, gold is sent in settlement of the balance, not because any change has taken place in its intrinsic value, *i.e.*, in its exchangeable relation to all other commodities, either in the exporting or in the importing country, but simply because it is employed as international currency, in which function it passes from hand to hand between persons residing in different countries, on precisely the same principles as it passes between individuals in the same country—in payment of debts ; and there is no more truth in the doctrine that gold flows from country to country only because of a difference in its value, than there would be in the assertion that it never passes from hand to hand, or from town to town, out of one county or parish, into another county or parish, except on account of differences in its intrinsic value. Reduced to its logical conclusions, the absolute erroneousness of the fundamental assumption upon which the monetary legislation of this great commercial country rests, is painfully apparent.

The following quotations will show that I am not combating a mere shadow of my own creation, but that the advocates of our present monetary system have actually been compelled by the irresistible force of logic to go to this extreme length in the direction of error.

Thus specie will be sent abroad to discharge a debt only when it is *superabundant*; only when it is the cheapest exportable commodity. — *Ricardo's Political Works*, p. 269.

Money is exported from the country in preference to other commodities only because money is in excess, and is therefore cheaper here than in other countries. But this excess of quantity is soon corrected, and the money of this country restored to an equality of value with the money of other countries by the export of gold, provided the place of the gold thus exported be not supplied by new issues of paper money. But if paper be not contracted on this principle, the security for the certain stoppage of the drain is lost.—*Lord Overstone's Evidence,* 1857.

Gold will not leave this country unless gold be *dearer* in some other country than it is in this.—*Sir Robert Peel's Speech in the House, May* 6, 1844, *on the introduction of the Bank Act.*

Bullion, like other commodities, is exported only when its exportation is profitable. It is never sent from England to France or America unless it is more valuable in those countries than here.—*M'Culloch's ' Wealth of Nations,'* p. 494.

Nothing could be more confident or candid than this, and yet it would be just as absurd, and no more so, to assert that none of us pay away gold except when we have an excess of it—more than we care to have—or know what to do with. We use it as currency, receive it and part with it as a medium of exchange, employ it as an instrument to facilitate exchanges, and part with it in paying off debts and in making purchases, not for the reason assigned theoretically, but in the practical discharge of obligations pure and simple. The debt is the immediate cause of the transfer—the gold is the means; and the transfer of the gold on the one hand, and the cancelment of the debt on the other, are the effects. It is precisely the same in international payments. It is true that in one case the gold crosses a frontier, in the other not, but this does not alter the case one iota, it does not transform the discharging of a debt, into an excess of gold.

A further inference may be deduced from the foregoing remarks. It is often supposed that gold is never exported unless to give a profit to those who despatch it. But this is manifestly a fallacious idea. The expression which is so often made use of, that the rates of exchange in any country are at such a point that no profit is to be made on shipment of gold to it must be carefully guarded from leading to a misconception. Such a fact is valuable to know, to a certain degree; but it does not prove that the despatch of bullion may not be natural and necessary nevertheless. It must be sent by those who are in debt to that country, if they cannot find bills. It is far more important to enquire, Is the balance of indebtedness also changed? The exchanges may remain exactly at specie point for a long time, offering no prospect of profit to any cambist, yet compelling the constant flow of bullion in order to discharge liabilities. It is not so superfluous as many might believe to dwell so frequently and strongly upon this point, because, as a matter of fact, language is constantly held, even among men who should be well versed in questions of this kind, which is practically at variance with the principles here put forth, though, in theory, they command immediate assent.—*Right Hon. G. J. Goschen—Theory of the Foreign Exchanges*, p. 116.

§ 6. This extraordinary error respecting the causes of outflows of gold was only equalled in absurdity by the long since exploded doctrine that

wealth consisted solely of money ; and the regulation of the currency by the foreign exchanges in
utter disregard of the fatal consequences to the
whole of our financial arrangements, and the important interests resting thereon, was not surpassed
in rank error by the mercantile system of trade
which aimed at insuring a constant influx of the
precious metals by encouraging exports, and
restricting and discouraging imports. Both sys-
tems rested upon an error respecting gold, and it
appears to me that the one doctrine was supple-
mentary to the other, and that they date from the
same period. Adam Smith gave the deathblow to
the one childish conceit, and it is really wonderful
how the other has so long eluded detection. It is
to be found in the writings of most of our eminent
political economists, and that conservative element
in opinions, which is in many respects so valuable,
naturally leads to great reliance being placed in
those who have once attained the position of
authorities on matters like this. Hence it is that
progress in the advance of truths is so slow; errors
having once gained root, long continuing to constitute the centre of that reasoning in a circle by
which all the other errors based upon them
are defended. And so it has been in this case.
At the present moment the errors with which we
are dealing are being defended by appeals to those
very authorities whom we have seen to be so utterly
at sea on the subject. It will serve to counteract

this tendency if I show how this deplorable fallacy arose.

I will again quote M'Culloch, and I may here observe that I do so simply because he is the clearest exponent of the doctrines; assisted in the construction of the system founded on them, and entered the lists in their defence after the crash of 1847. The following quotations are extracted out of the edition published after that date :—

At page 480 of his 5th edition of 'Adam Smith's Wealth of Nations,' he lays down the principles by which the value of money is determined, when every one is allowed to bring additional supplies of *gold* and *silver* to market, unrestricted, or subject to no restraint or monopoly. He very correctly points out that under these circumstances their value would be determined by the universal laws of supply and demand, and takes the precaution to show, that notwithstanding this, '*the commercial intercourse established amongst the remotest quarters of the world has distributed gold and silver, so that their value in one country differs but little from their value in another; and while their great durability prevents any sudden diminution in their quantity, the immense surface over which they are spread, and the various purposes to which they are applied, render the effect of a considerably increased supply hardly sensible.*'

He then, in the next section, proceeds to lay down the laws by which its value would be determined if the power to supply money was placed under restraint; and it is here that we find the fundamental fallacy. We are now in that dangerous region of hypothesis in which, if the necessary conditions are only granted, anything can be proved. It is a region in which the best of us are liable to soar far away above the world of facts, and in which fancy, supposition, speculative thought, are nurtured and fed.

'*Whenever the supply of money is limited, he states, its value varies in the inverse ratio of its quantity as compared with the quantity of commodities brought to market, or with the business it has to perform. If, on the one hand, double the usual supply of commodities were brought to market in a country with a limited currency, their money price would be reduced a half; and if, on the other hand, only half the usual supply of commodities were brought to market, their price would be doubled; and this, whether the cost of production was increased or diminished. Sovereigns, shillings, livres, dollars, &c., would then merely constitute mere tickets or counters, to be used in computing the value of property, and in transferring it from one individual to another. And as small tickets or counters would serve for that purpose quite as well as large ones, it is unquestionably true, that a debased currency may, by first reducing, and then limiting its quantity, be made to circulate at the value it would bear, were the power to supply it unrestricted, and were it of legal weight and fineness; and by still limiting its quantity, it may be made to pass at any higher value. . . . It appears, therefore, that whatever be the matter of which money is made, and however destitute of intrinsic value, it is yet possible, by sufficiently limiting its quantity, to raise its value to any conceivable extent.*'—M'Culloch's '*Wealth of Nations*,' p. 482.

He then proceeds to state that this is strictly
applicable to an inconvertible paper currency; but
not to a freely supplied metallic currency. Several
sections on other matters then intervene, in the course
of which he enunciates the erroneous proposition,
amongst others, that a fall in the foreign exchanges
and an efflux of bullion, would, under an inconvertible paper currency, be a conclusive proof that the
efflux was caused by a redundancy of currency—
utterly forgetful of the fact, that even under such
a currency the numerous causes of drains would still
be in operation, and that the mere fact of a drain
existing would, in itself, be no proof whatever that
it had arisen from any particular one of a number
of possible causes. In point of fact the proposition
is doubly erroneous. The depreciation in the
currency, which is put forward as the sole cause of
all drains, would really be no such thing. The
actual cause would be international indebtedness,
and this might arise from any one of the innumerable possible causes. Although an inordinate increase in the issue of inconvertible notes might
lead to depreciation, yet it could not in itself create
international indebtedness, and could not, therefore,
be the cause of the outflow of gold. An outflow
of gold might arise from any one of a number of
possible causes, and the mere outflow would not
prove that it arose from the one universal cause
assigned; and, *vice versa*, a depreciation in the
currency might exist without an outflow of gold

going on. The rate of exchange would indicate the presence of any depreciation, and I have no doubt this is how the fallacy arose; it is one of confusion. The depreciation being always added to the REAL exchange, the fact of the exchange being adverse beyond the cost of the transmission of bullion, would indicate that the currency was depreciated, and the extent of the depreciation could be ascertained by deducting from the adverse premium the usual cost and expenses; the residue would give the deprecia-tion. The adverse premium would, however, simply indicate the depreciation, but not only would the depreciation not cause an immediate and continuous export of gold, as is erroneously assumed, but it might, and, as a matter of fact, has, repeatedly existed in the face of an inflow of gold. It is true that both the depreciation and the inflow of gold might arise from the same cause, from an extraordinary expenditure by the Government, for instance, as was the case in this country at the opening of the present century; but they would stand in the relation to one another, not of cause and effect, but as coinci-dent effects arising from the same common cause. If the increase in the issue of paper led to the dis-placement of gold in the channels of circulation, and the gold, which was rendered available, was exported, the export would have been rendered possible by the operation, but would not have been caused by it. The export would have been caused by the in-ternational indebtedness of the country having been

increased by some of the numerous possible causes
pointed out in the preceding pages. If the depreciation indicated by the exchanges pervaded the
gold as well as the paper, then in that case it would
undoubtedly lead to an export of gold, and that,
whether the paper currency was convertible or inconvertible; and this is the rock upon which the
political economists have stranded. They have
treated a depreciation *between* gold and paper as
synonymous with a depreciation *in* gold and paper.
But even although such a general depreciation in a
convertible currency would at once lead to an outflow of gold, yet still an outflow of gold would not
be proof that such depreciation did exist, for, as has
been so frequently pointed out, the outflow might
arise from a number of causes, and it is a violation
of the rules of reasoning to argue one particular
cause from the presence of an effect common to a
number of causes. Whilst, therefore, it is quite
within the range of possibility that any outflow of
gold which may be taking place, may be the effect
of a depreciation in the currency, yet, as there are
a number of possible causes, the probabilities are
immense against its arising from this one particular
cause assigned, and the proposition to the contrary
is a remarkable instance of error. It is a fallacy of
treating a particular as an universal, an error all the
more glaring from the fact that the particular selected
was one of a large number of well-known causes,
and was the most improbable cause of all. If there

had been a small number of causes only, and if all the
others, except the one selected, had been of a very
weak, faint, and remote character, then in that case
the fallacy would have been excusable, and we could
have understood the one powerful cause eclipsing
its brethren and becoming in time to be regarded as
the sole and universal cause, for that is a class of
fallacy very general, and to be met with in all directions, but in this case no such defence is possible.
That M'Culloch, who is one of the highest authorities
we have on commercial, statistical, and economical
questions, should have had the misfortune of falling
into such a transparent error, is most deplorable.

The proposition is not applicable to either a convertible or an inconvertible currency. Although
the outflow of gold at any time *may* possibly proceed
from a depreciation in the currency, yet the mere
presence of the outflow would not prove that it
actually did so; it could, at the most, only serve to
confirm the proof, if sufficient was forthcoming, and
even in such an improbable event, it would not be
necessary to take legislative measures for the contraction of the currency; the outflow itself would
reduce and contract it on the one hand, and as has
been already shown, the laws of supply and demand
would speedily bring other corrective forces into
operation, and the irresistible conclusion is, that the
fallacy, and the machinery built upon it, is altogether an unfortunate blunder. Whilst it would be
an economical heresy to deny the possibility of such

a general depreciation of the currency arising, yet the probabilities against it are immense, and it is quite capable of demonstration, that if one hundred million of gold was poured into this country to-morrow it would produce no appreciable effect upon its *intrinsic* value, *i.e.*, upon general prices. Two or three of our friendly powers, would, I venture to say, offer to relieve us of it, with pleasure. Turkey would be in the market for a little slice of it at once, and our friends of South America would be quite demonstrative in the warmth of their friendship. There are so many outlets for capital, that we manage to go on year after year adding to our accumulated wealth without producing any appreciable effect on values, and yet in the face of this we have gone on believing that every paltry import or export of gold affected its intrinsic value, and that variations in its value were the sole and only cause of its international movements. Involved in a vicious circle of reasoning we have quietly gone on sleeping over the error, awaking only every now and then when it was producing its baneful effects. Principles when sound are truly priceless, but when unsound and false they scourge their victims for their blind devotion.

It will be observed that even if the proposition had been applicable to an inconvertible currency, yet that the hypotheses on which this ratio doctrine is based are altogether inapplicable to our convertible currency. Under a gold and paper currency like ours, under which the paper is convertible into gold, and the supply of gold is subject to no restriction or monopoly, all parties being freely allowed to import gold *ad libitum*, and to have it coined at the Mint, free of charge—under this currency the facts are exactly the reverse of those from which the hypothetical conclusions are deduced; and yet M'Culloch positively leaps across the boundary line which divides convertible and inconvertible currencies, and commits the unfortunate error of applying to our convertible currency the conclusions drawn from these inapplicable hypotheses.

This error lands him in the erroneous conclusion that even under our convertible currency—' the fact that the exchange has fallen and that bullion is being exported, proves incontrovertibly that it is redundant; and that consequently the Directors of the Bank of England should immediately set about contracting their issues, *to prevent the exhaustion of their coffers* ' (p. 494).

These are the unfortunate errors upon which the monetary system of England rests at the present moment; and this is the purely fictitious danger out of fear of which we periodically plunge into the depths of financial disorganization, loss, and disaster !

A further fallacy still was necessary to complete this Palace of Error, and it was readily adopted. During the period of suspension of cash payments; paper currency, on the one hand, and Bonaparte, on the other, were regarded as the special and par-

E

ticular foes of England. If anything miscarried in
our diplomatic enterprises—and diplomats never
before or since had so lively a time of it—Bonaparte was at once said to be at the bottom of it,
and he was regarded with such a feeling of dread
and aversion, that we were at all times ready to ex-
pend our blood and treasure in thwarting him. And
so with paper currency. If the Government drained
the country of its treasure for the payment of sub-
sidies, and flooded the country with inconvertible
paper in its reckless expenditure, the fault, it was
said, lay in the paper, and not in the action of the
Government. If corn went up, the consumers said
it was the paper ; if down, the farmers also said it
was the paper: nothing was too great or too small
for the unfortunate paper to bear, and on the paper
every grievance was put accordingly. Over-issue
was the peg on which every grievance was hung up ;
and as there no doubt was a modicum of truth in
the cry, it speedily took possession of the national
mind. But whatever substratum of truth there was
in this cry of over-issue, it was applicable only to an
inconvertible paper currency ; but instead of being
abandoned on the resumption of cash payments, it
was firmly adhered to, and so it comes to pass that
it forms a part of the foundation of our monetary
system at the present moment. It was loudly asserted up to 1844 that the mismanagement of the
currency was still the bane of the country, the cause
of every disaster, and the fruitful source of all evil.

Every outflow of gold was ascribed to an excessive issue of notes, and up to the present moment it is held that such is the case. We shall have occasion to go fully into this question further on, but it will be as well just to glance at it in this place.

The error of supposing that the Bank can, under a convertible currency, keep out more notes than are required, and thereby depress the exchangeable value of the whole currency, is apparent on the slightest reflection. Even granting that it is in the power of a bank to enlarge the issue of notes by fostering a demand, still any such issue, as well as any other arising from a demand, whether fostered or not, would simply meet the demand, and so far from producing an alteration in the exchangeable value of the whole convertible currency, would positively prevent the demand creating any such effect. If the demand proved to be permanent, then the increased supply would likewise be permanent, and would simply meet it and prevent any fluctuation in its exchangeable value arising. If, on the other hand, the demand proved to be temporary, the enlarged supply would likewise be temporary, for the notes would be returned upon the issuers the instant they ceased to be required. This is so clear that it only requires to be stated to command immediate assent, and yet a vast mass of sophistry and error has been constructed on this very supposition, which has perhaps done more to obscure and confuse the whole subject than all the other errors put together. The error is like one of those bubbles by children blown, which burst on the slightest touch.

But, it will be contended, the increased supply of currency would not merely satisfy the demand for it, but would also create a demand in the market of commodities, and thereby tend to raise general prices and lower the exchangeable value of money. The first answer to this is that the power of banks to foster a demand is extremely limited, the fact that banks have under the present system frequently the privilege to issue a large additional amount of notes, without the power, proving this; and the second, and more conclusive answer, is, that if we are to attempt by legislation to destroy everything which has a *tendency* to raise prices, we shall have a very pretty task on our hands. Why, everything which tends to increase the demand has precisely the same tendency; the whole of the numerous forms of credit, of which banknotes constitute only an insignificant portion, possess the same tendency, and it is not a mere question of note issues, but a question of supply and demand, to the operation of the laws of which we may safely leave the matter. I have already had occasion to point out that even if general prices were to be raised by an excessive extension of the use of credit in the shape of notes, or otherwise, by speculation or by any other temporary cause, that such a rise would be corrected in the ordinary course of mercantile dealings by the operation of the ever-active laws of supply and demand—laws operating

not here only but universally—and that it is altogether
a mistake to take scientific precautions for the due
break-down of the whole of our financial machinery
whenever a severe drain arises. A question like
this, underlying as it does the whole range of subjects embraced by the science of political economy,
cannot be settled satisfactorily if we adhere to the
narrow spirit of exaggerating every tendency, rushing to extremes, and shutting out from consideration
the general laws to which any particular tendency is
subject. We must extend the scope of our vision
over the whole range of laws, tendencies, and
counter-tendencies, by which final and actual results are produced, and not attempt to settle the
question on a limited basis, for any such settlement
cannot, except by the merest chance, fail to be delusive and erroneous. It is the very essence of
scientific accuracy in the collection of truths out of
a wide range of data to take every fact into consideration and to allow to it its due weight in the
general conclusion ; but on this unfortunate subject it
has been the rule to treat particulars as universals,
to push single and isolated tendencies to the utmost
possibilities, and then to adopt the conclusion so
arrived at as a universal truth. This is so diametrically opposed to all the laws of reason and investigation, that its very incredibility has protected it
from suspicion, and Sir Robert Peel was led into
adopting the so-called scientific truths without for
one moment doubting their soundness. The very

concatenation of authority by which they were up-
held served to cover an almost transparent error.
As already stated, I shall have occasion further on,
when I come to the question of over-issues, to deal
finally and conclusively with this question of the
relation between currency and prices, and shall then
show that prices, are governed by the laws of supply
and demand; that amongst the numerous and
powerful forces which go to make up the aggregate
demand at any given moment, currency holds a very
secondary place ; and that under a convertible paper
currency the fluctuation in the amount of currency
in circulation is the effect and not the cause of the
fluctuations in prices and the extent and activity of
trade.

The utter absurdity of this ratio doctrine is
clearly shown by the fact that if it is true that a
reduction in the quantity of the circulation to the
extent of one-half, will raise the value of the remaining half to the original value of the whole, then, by
simply repeating the process, a single atom could be
raised to any value we assume.   If, for instance, the
original quantity was equal in value to a million
quarters of grain, then, by the process of reducing
the quantity, either gradually or at once, to a single
atom, this atom, according to the doctrine, would be
raised to the original value of the whole mass—one
million quarters of grain !   And on the other hand,
by doubling the quantity, the value of the original
quantity would be reduced by one-half !   Could

anything be more preposterous or out of place in the treatment of a science dealing with such practical subjects as political economy does?

If anything further was required to prove the unsoundness of the doctrine, I cannot conceive that any more complete proof on the point could be adduced than the conclusions at which Mr. Tooke arrived, after making the most complete investigation of it ever conducted.

The conclusion, then, at which we arrive is, shortly, that the total stock of gold in various forms in Europe and America at the close of 1848 was 560 millions sterling, and that the *aggregate* of the annual additions to that total stock from California, Australia, and Russia, during the eight years 1849–56, have been 174 millions sterling, or equal (as already explained) to an addition of 27 per cent.—*Tooke's ' History of Prices,'* vol. vi. p. 154.

It has been made apparent, that at the entrance of this ninth year, 1857, after the commencement of the great influx in 1848, it is impossible to affirm that the range of the general prices has been sensibly raised, by the mere operation in the form of metallic money, of 160 or 170 millions of new gold introduced into the commercial world. It has appeared that all the instances of an important variation in price, comparing 1857 with 1851, admit of being accounted for by circumstances affecting the supply or the demand.—*Vide* p. 224.

As a matter of fact, we have seen that it is not true that even an increase of one-third of the quantity of metallic money has led to a corresponding increase of general prices; nor, in the case of large groups of commodities, to any increase of price whatever; but on the contrary, that prices have rather sunk to a lower than risen to a higher level. As a matter of general reasoning

it may be said that the abstract argument which urges
the constant dependence of the range of prices on the
quantity of money is, on several grounds, a conspicuous
example of the fallacious inferences which arise from the
treatment of economical questions in the same manner as
problems in geometry.—*Vide* p. 194.

§ 7. Not only, however, is this '*ratio doctrine*'
inapplicable to our convertible currency, but, as we
have already seen, it is not even applicable to an inconvertible paper currency. The value of such a currency depends upon a variety of causes, the credit of
the issuers obviously being one of the most important.
The moment a State in bad credit, and whose interest-
bearing obligations are at a heavy discount, reverts
to an inconvertible paper currency, the value of
the State issues immediately sinks below par, even
although the quantity in circulation is not increased.
On the other hand, a State in first-class credit may
suspend specie payments without any such effect
following. If the notes are received in payment of
taxes, and are not issued in excess of the currency
requirements of the country, they will maintain par
value for an indefinite length of time. If they are
convertible into government stock, and received by
the Government in payment for interest-bearing
bonds, then their value cannot fall much below the
value of the bonds, and it is well known that the
value of government bonds is not determined on
this ratio doctrine, otherwise what would have been
the value of our funded debt, or of those of the

American and French Governments at the present moment? Positively, the idea won't bear looking at, and how on earth the political economists came to admit such an absurdly hypothetical theory into their writings on so practical a subject as political economy, I cannot understand.

France affords the most recent case in point, and the most complete confirmation of the truths here laid down. The notes of the Bank of France in circulation increased from 1,470,193,000 francs, at which they stood on 21st July, 1870, at the outbreak of the war, to 3,012,536,770 francs, on 13th November, 1873, which was the highest point reached, and yet there existed no depreciation in the French currency. According to the ratio doctrine an enormous depreciation ought to have existed, but did not. And not only was there no depreciation in the paper, but there was also no depreciation in the whole currency, in the metal and paper, as there should have been according to the ratio doctrine. If there had been any such general depreciation it would, if sufficient to cover the cost of the transmission of bullion and yield a profit, have caused an immediate and continuous export of the metallic portion of the currency.

Now, although a large quantity of gold was exported by France in the course of these financial operations, yet this export was not caused by a depreciation of the currency, for no such cause was in existence. It was not caused by the issue of

paper, as the doctrinaires assert, but, as a matter
of fact, the issue of paper and the export of gold
were both effects of the same common cause, both
arose out of the payment of the War indemnity.
The innumerable causes which affect international
indebtedness were in active operation throughout
the period, but in addition to the ordinary causes
there was that powerful disturbing element, the
unfortunate War indemnity. And even this cause
was, to a very considerable extent, controllable. If
the French Government had so determined, they
could have denuded the country of the whole of its
metallic currency, but they were clever financiers,
and instead of doing so they respected the central
reserve, and preserved the country from the dis-
honesty of a depreciated currency. Instead of
emptying the coffers of the Bank of France and
issuing an inordinate amount of paper in order to
obtain the money free of interest, as we did at the
opening of the present century, and as the United
States did during their civil war, they adopted the
wiser policy of limiting the issue of paper to the
actual requirements of the country, and honestly
borrowed the rest on interest-bearing bonds. It is
true that by issuing notes of lower denominations
they displaced a large amount of coin which was in
the channels of circulation, and rendered it available
for the urgent wants of the country, but this operation, while it led to the doubling of the amount of
notes in circulation, did not increase the volume

of the whole currency, the paper simply replacing the coin. Fortunately for this country they encroached, in the autumn of 1873, to the extent of a few millions sterling further on their central bullion reserve ; had they not done so, another financial disaster would most probably have been registered on our wreck-strewn annals.

The great danger of an inconvertible currency is that the Government may be driven by its necessities or induced by temptation to *force* a larger amount of currency into circulation than is required. The moment the boundary line has been passed, a small additional amount will not merely act according to the ratio doctrine, but in a constantly increasing ratio, within the limits previously pointed out. But it is of supreme importance to bear in mind that it is only under an inconvertible currency that currency can be so forced into circulation *and kept there*. Not being convertible into gold, the door is shut against its returning upon the issuers except in the payment of taxes, and where an extraordinary expenditure is taking place, as is generally the case, the payments exceed the receipts, and a redundant amount of paper can be poured into the channels of circulation and forcibly kept there, but under a convertible currency like ours, any excess of paper is returned upon the issuers the moment it arises.

The reason why the French currency was not depreciated by this gigantic operation was (1) because it was not forced into circulation and forcibly kept there beyond the requirements of the country, and (2) because a large bullion reserve was throughout retained. On November 3, 1873, when the note issues reached the highest point, France had still a central bullion reserve of 731,575,853 francs (28,970,000l.), which very materially consolidated and protected the national credit. The operation was conducted with consummate skill, and redounds with credit to the French financiers, and it completely overthrows the erroneous opinions which are current amongst us on this subject.

§ 8. We have now completed the examination of this extraordinary assumption, that all drains of gold arise from a redundancy and depreciation in our currency, and with its destruction the whole theory on which the present principle of monetary legislation is based falls to the ground. It is the keystone of the whole disastrous policy, and has constituted the sole ground why that policy has not been abandoned years ago. And not only is the assumption utterly false and preposterous as applied to our mixed currency, but a moment's calm reflection discloses that it is not even applicable to a purely metallic currency, and that the proposition to the contrary is nothing more than a rash, false, gratuitous, and deplorable assumption. In such a typical currency, the numerous causes which at present bring about exports of gold in the settlement of international indebtedness would operate precisely as they do at present, and the mere export of gold would afford no proof whatever that every export arose from its superabundance in the exporting country. The very foundation stone of the whole theory is, like the superstructure, false and absurd. It affords a signal instance of the folly of that love of generalizing which appears to afford such delight to a certain class of minds, which love to treat the subjects with which they are dealing in a philosophical manner. A smattering of philosophy raises them, they think, at once above the common mass of humanity who are contented with facts, and when requested to descend into this lower world and account for the facts clashing with the theories, they exclaim, with supreme contempt, that they take their stand on theory, and that if facts do not agree with it, why, so much the worse for the facts. Sound generalization is invaluable, but Bacon would appear to have written in vain so far as this branch of human knowledge is concerned. Induction, he pointed out, is the process on which all sound investigation should be conducted and on which generalization should be constructed; but in this case we have been content to adhere to the old source of error, deduction, and to legislate on a wild hypothesis, without taking the ordinary precaution of testing its soundness by comparing it with facts.

A purely metallic currency is a type of perfection in this respect, and in this respect only, viz. its absolute conformity in value to the standard of value,

which it would at the same time constitute and
represent, but in so far as its inconveniences and the
evils which would arise from any insufficiency in its
quantity to act as a medium of exchange, whether
such deficiency was permanent or temporary, are
concerned, it is a type to be carefully avoided. The
object to be aimed at with respect to a mixed currency is not to make it conform in its fluctuations in
its quantity to the inconvenient fluctuations of a
purely metallic currency, but to ensure its conformity in value to the standard, and if under a
purely metallic currency the value of the standard
would, owing to imperfect financial machinery, have
fluctuated in a violent manner, as these gentlemen
erroneously assume it would, then such violent fluctuations should be avoided as far as possible, and not
copied. Such fluctuations in the standard would at
any time be an intolerable evil, but at the present
day, when floating financial transactions have assumed such enormous proportions, they would be
absolutely fatal, and to aim at ensuring them would
be madness. I repeat, and it cannot be too carefully borne in mind, that what we have to aim at on
this point is to ensure the conformity in value of the
paper portion of the currency to the standard, and
the most simple, and at the same time most certain
means of doing this is to provide for its convertibility
into gold. There are no doubt other and more
economical means of doing this, for it would be
quite possible to make an inconvertible currency

conform in value to the standard, but such a currency is so liable to abuse, and has actually been so much abused in the past, owing partly to the unfortunate circumstances under which it has invariably been had recourse to, that public opinion is not yet ripe for such an extension of the principle of economy in that direction. The advocates of a purely metallic currency as a type to be aimed at have pushed the idea too far, and have treated value and quantity as synonymous terms. Had they started with a sound and clear conception of the type, they would never have fallen into so outrageous an error. They would have seen that we require no hypothetical type for our guidance. We possess in this country a definite and solid standard of value, and what we have to do is, to see that our currency conforms in *value* to that standard. If we build prudently and circumspectly on this foundation, we shall stand a fair chance of possessing a sound and safe monetary system, a much better chance than if we again build upon hypotheses totally inapplicable to the condition of things and to the world of facts by which we are surrounded.

CHAPTER II.

PRACTICAL WORKING OF THE SYSTEM FOUNDED ON THIS ERRONEOUS PRINCIPLE.

§ 1. HAVING now made a complete survey of the astoundingly erroneous principle of monetary legislation of this the great financial centre of the world, and fathomed the wondrous sea of fallacy in profound depths never before by plummet sounded, we will proceed to look into the practical working of the monetary system founded upon this mountain of error. We shall have to widen the field of observation considerably in order to give stability to the inductions deducible from the facts, but having discovered the key to the solution of the problem, we shall find the main truths lying on the surface of events, and shall have no difficulty in extricating ourselves out of this maze of error, and bringing to a close this panic period of finance. I beg to direct particular attention to the circumstance that in every instance we meet with the same important fact—that the remedy was found in the abandonment of the one principle of regulation, and the adoption, in every case, of the contrary and directly opposite principle, viz. that of supporting and protecting our financial arrangements from the disturbing influences, and the abandonment of the policy of forcibly contracting the currency, or regulating it by the foreign exchanges.

The first instance of this to which it is necessary to refer occurred in 1793. The state of things on the Continent was very unsettled, the great war was impending, and, a heavy drain of the precious metals taking place, the directors acted upon the restrictive principle, and violently contracted their issues and accommodation. They were so infatuated with the theory that they refused to comply with the request of the Government to relieve the pressure by the adoption of a liberal policy, and so Government came forward to the relief of commercial credit, and authorised the advance, upon approved securities, of 5,000,000*l.* exchequer bills. This measure completely restored confidence, and dissolved the pressure.

In 1796, the Bank had again recourse to the restrictive policy, and again the pressure created was so great, that on the 2nd April the merchants and bankers of London held a meeting, and petitioned the Bank to afford more liberal accommodation.

In 1797 a loan was made to the Emperor of Germany, heavy war expenditure was entered into, and the balance of international indebtedness having turned against us, a heavy demand for bullion for export sprung up, and the Bank, endeavouring to

F

adhere to the restrictive policy, reduced the note issues from 10,550,830*l.* to 8,540,250*l.* between the 21st January and the 25th February. The pressure created was so intense that an internal drain and panic arose, and specie payments were suspended on the 27th February. The policy was again abandoned, and by an extension of the issues of 2,000,000*l.* in one week the panic was allayed.

The Governor and Deputy-Governor of the Bank assured the Bullion Committee in 1810 that the distress of 1793 and 1796-7 was undoubtedly produced by the restrictive action of the Bank, and that the directors regretted having enforced it. The Committee expressly condemned the policy, and laid down the principle that a liberal policy is the only means of preserving confidence. They condemned any arbitrary limitation of the power of the Bank to issue, and particularly pointed out the necessity of the Bank being able to support public credit in periods of alarm and pressure.

A very urgent demand for guineas, though arising not from the high price of gold and the state of the exchange, but from a fear of invasion, occurred in 1793 and also in 1797, and in each of these periods the Bank restrained their discounts, and consequently also the amount of their notes, very much below the demand of the merchants. Your Committee question the policy of thus limiting the accommodation in a period of alarm, unaccompanied with an unfavourable exchange and high price of bullion ; but they consider the conduct of the Bank at the two last-mentioned periods as affording illustration of their general disposition, antecedently to 1797, to contract

their loans and their paper when they found their gold to
be taken from them. . . . So long as the paper of the
Bank was convertible into specie at the will of the holder,
it was enough, both for the safety of the Bank and the
public interest in what regarded its circulating medium,
that the directors attended only to the character and
quality of the bills discounted as real ones, and payable
at fixed and short periods. . . . The late Governor and
Deputy-Governor of the Bank stated to your Committee,
that they and many of the directors are now satisfied,
from the experience of the year 1797, that the diminution
of their notes in that emergency increased the public
distress, an opinion in the correctness of which your Committee entirely concur. . . . Your Committee are clearly
of opinion that, although it ought to be the general
policy of the Bank directors to diminish their paper in
the event of the *long continuance of a high price of
bullion* and a *very* unfavourable exchange, yet it is
effectual to the commercial interest of the country, and
to the general fulfilment of those mercantile engagements
which a free issue of paper may have occasioned, that the
accustomed degree of accommodation to merchants should
not be suddenly and materially reduced; and if a general
and serious difficulty or apprehension on this subject
should arise, it may, in the judgment of your Committee,
be counteracted without danger, and with advantage to
the public, by a liberality in the issue of Bank of England
paper, proportioned to the urgency of the particular
occasion.—*Bullion Report,* 1810. [The Bullion Committee here recommend contraction under a particular
condition of things, and expressly condemn it under a
state of things such as at present exists. The fundamental error of the present system consists in applying to
a CONVERTIBLE currency a rule which is partially applicable
only to an INCONVERTIBLE currency.]

In 1825, another striking example of the disastrous effects of the policy occurred. The restrictive action of the Bank was so severe that deputations from Manchester, Edinburgh, and Glasgow waited upon the Bank to request the abandonment of the policy. At the last moment, when our commercial and credit system was on the point of collapsing, the directors again abandoned it. Their issues, which had been reduced from 19,686,570l. to 17,477,290l. between the 15th October and the 3rd December, were enlarged to 25,611,800l. by the 24th December, and their discounts were increased from 7,500,000l. to 15,000,000l. between the 8th and 29th December. By these prompt measures the panic was dispelled.

Panic of 1839.—The drain set in in October, 1838, and the bullion, which on the 26th of that month amounted to 9,350,000l., was reduced to 2,406,000l. by the 3rd of September, 1839. This protracted drain was produced by extensive purchases in this country of American securities, railway expenditure, and the heavy imports of corn.

Towards the middle of the drain it was intensified by the state of alarm on the Continent regarding the ability of the Bank to maintain cash payments, and in consequence of this, a large amount of bills drawn on this country were suddenly thrown upon the market and discounted. On the 20th June the Bank rate was raised from 5 to $5\frac{1}{2}$ per cent., and on the 1st August to 6 per cent. Attempting to adhere to the principle and contract the circulation, the directors, in August, sold a large portion of its public securities, and afterwards tried to sell a portion of the Dead Weight, but not being able to obtain a satisfactory price, they borrowed 750,000*l.* exchequer bills from the East India Company, a portion of which they sold. Finding that the drain continued and the pressure increased, the Bank at last abandoned the principle of regulation; and to prevent the total suspension of commerce, opened credits on the Continent, and by that means operated directly on the exchanges. Bills were drawn at three months' date by Messrs. Barings on Paris, and by other houses on Amsterdam and Hamburgh, to the extent of 2,500,000*l.*, for which the Bank undertook to provide, and guaranteed by a deposit of a portion of the dead weight. These bills being thrown into the market, at once arrested the drain, and the country was saved. The bills were settled partly by the transmission of *bonâ fide* bills and partly by bullion, and were completely liquidated by April, 1840.

Here again we have a repetition of events. The drain, produced by specific causes, brought into operation the restrictive principle, and pressure and panic ensued; the principle was abandoned, credit supported, panic arrested, and confidence restored.

In the year 1844 a change was made in the method of applying this disastrous principle. Previous to that year the directors had acted upon it voluntarily. They professed to regulate their issues

according to the foreign exchanges, but had found
it impracticable to do so on all occasions, and those
departures from the policy were now made the
ground for the passing of the Act of 1844. It was
contended by the advocates of the system of regulation that the pressures and panics to which the
country was subject arose from the imperfect manner
in which the principle had been applied. It was
shown that the note circulation did not fluctuate
with the bullion reserve, but that their variations
were often inverse to each other, the one enlarging
when the other diminished. Parliament, therefore,
determined to apply the principle systematically, and
to bring it into action at an earlier stage of the
drains. They proceeded on the assumptions that the
principle of regulation was sound; that pressures
were unavoidable; that, to secure the cessation of
drains a reduction in the currency was indispensable; and that, by early and gradual pressures, late
and severe ones would be avoided.

And so in 1844 it was decreed that this pseudo-
principle of monetary legislation should be forcibly
placed into mechanical operation. The doctrinaires
were in the ascendant, and the Legislature, confounded by the conflicting theories, determined to
afford their theory a full and fair trial. The result is soon told. Like a blazing meteor the system has ever since been rushing through the financial sky, with ruin and destruction in its train, scat-
tering disaster around it wherever it has been

brought into close proximity to our financial machinery. The child of error, it has been a scourge to the nation, an avenger of the immutable truths which have so long lain neglected within our grasp.

In accordance with the principle of regulation based upon such utterly false assumptions, and for the express purpose of making the currency fluctuate with the foreign exchanges, fixed limits were placed on the note issues of the country bankers, and provision made for their ultimate extinction. The Bank of England was divided into the issue and banking departments, and a limit placed on its power to issue notes against securities. That limit is at the present moment 15,000,000*l.*, and all notes issued beyond that amount must be represented by bullion in the issue department. As bullion flows into the coffers of the Bank the limit of issue enlarges, and *vice versa* as bullion flows out. Proceeding on the additional false assumption that the inflow and efflux of gold in the Bank corresponded with the movements of the foreign exchanges, and profoundly oblivious to the patent fact that there is such a thing as very wide fluctuations in the internal currency requirements of the country, they lulled themselves and the country into a state of serene repose, confident that the disturbing elements had been for ever chained down and finally repressed. The goal of monetary science had at last been reached. Let us proceed to examine the results of this brilliant victory.

The Bank's reserve having by the latter part of
1847 been considerably reduced by a drain, created
principally by the heavy importation of provisions
consequent upon the deficient harvest and the failure
in the potato crop, the mercantile community became
alarmed. They saw that if the system was adhered
to, and the reserve continued to diminish, the Bank
would be compelled to contract its accommodation,
and very probably have to suspend payment in the
banking department, and they therefore endeavoured to prepare for the impending danger by
enlarging their available means. It was no groundless fear which seized the community, but one
created by a stern reality. Owing to the Act of
1844, the available reserve of the Bank to meet the
demand for discounts and deposits was, on the 23rd
of October, only 1,994,516*l.*, although the total
amount of bullion in the hands of the Bank was
8,759,937*l.*, the bulk of it being locked up in the
Issue Department. All engaged in trade, and dependent on credit, suddenly found the usual and
indispensable facilities contracted, and likely to be
totally withdrawn, and each hastened to provide
against the danger, and thereby aggravated it.
Confidence disappearing, there was a complete dead
lock, and a destructive panic raged. The difficulties
of the situation were increasing every moment, and
the panic was rapidly spreading throughout the whole
community, when, on the 25th October, the Government suspended the restrictive clauses of the Act,

and requested the Bank to afford liberal accommodation to the public. The panic immediately vanished, and our monetary machinery was again set in motion.

Money was hoarded to a considerable extent, so much so that, notwithstanding the notes and coin issued to the public in October exceeded by 4,000,000*l.* or 5,000,000*l.* the amount in August, still the general complaint was of a scarcity. of money. Credit was so entirely destroyed that houses trading to distant countries, carrying on their business through the means of credit by a renewal of their acceptances as they became due, were no longer able to meet their engagements, and were forced to stop payment. This was the state of things previous to the issuing of the Government letter in October.—*Lords' Report—Evidence of Governor and Deputy-Governor of Bank of England,* 1847–8.

The Committee have consequently felt it to be their duty to enquire into the course pursued by the Bank acting under the provisions of the 7 and 8 Vict., c. 32, and they have come to the conclusion that the recent panic was *materially aggravated by the operation of that statute*, and by the proceedings of the Bank itself. This effect may be traced directly to the Act of 1844, in the legislative restriction imposed on the means of accommodation, whilst a large amount of bullion was held in the coffers of the Bank, and during a time of favourable exchanges; and it may be traced to the same cause indirectly, as a consequence of great fluctuations in the rate of discount, and of capital previously advanced at an unusually low rate of interest.

If the Committee considered the Act of 1844, which they desire to be amended, as far as its restrictive clauses are concerned, was essential to the practical convertibility of the banknote, they would hesitate in recommending any change. But it should never be forgotten that the liability of the Bank consists in its deposits as well as in its promissory notes. The legal obligation to discharge both is the same. The failure of either would be equally fatal. . . . It appears impossible at once to defend the restrictive provisions of the Act, and to justify the letter which in this respect abrogated or at least suspended those very restrictive provisions. The Committee consider that those restrictions materially aggravated the pressure, and produced the panic of October 1847.—*Lords' Report*, 1848.

As Mr. Adam Hodgson, one of the directors of the Bank of Liverpool, stated before the Commons' Committee of 1847, ' the whole mischief was the want of confidence ; and confidence was at once restored by the letter.' Mr. Chas. Turner, M.P., J. H. Palmer, director of the Bank of England, and other witnesses, pointed out the same important fact. It was confidence and not capital that was required. The quantity of capital in the country was the same immediately after the suspension of the restrictive clauses of the Act as it was before ; but confidence at once assumed an entirely different phase, as is so graphically indicated by the following :—

Before two o'clock this relaxing letter had come down, and very generally the orders for money were withdrawn ; they said, ' We do not want the money now—we do not want the money now—there is no occasion to pay it.' Sums of money were immediately offered us, and people began to have confidence in the use of the notes which they had. Before the week was over we had to go and ask the Bank, as a favour, to let us repay the money we had borrowed.—*S. Gurney—Commons' Report*, 1847.

The next repetition of these disastrous events

took place in 1857. On the 11th November the reserve available to meet all demands for deposits and
discounts was only 1,462,153*l.*, although the total
amount of bullion in the Bank was 7,170,000*l.*, and as
this reserve was being rapidly reduced, the pressure
merged into a complete panic. All the attendant
disasters were again witnessed, and again the remedy
was found in the suspension of the restrictive clauses
of the Act and the abandonment of the system of
regulation. In order to preserve commerce from
complete disorganisation, the Government was compelled to break the law by which that system was
enforced.

In consequence of the necessity for indemni-
fying the Government for having suspended the
Bank Act, Parliament was called together on 3rd
December, 1857.

During the debate in the House of Lords, the Earl of
Derby said that he had had thirty-six years of political
life, abounding in periods of strong political excitement,
of commercial distress and agricultural distress, of dangerous wars, of internal tumults—a revolutionary spirit
abroad, religious agitations at home; but all these had
come singly. Now all calamities had come together in
most disastrous complication. The chief object of their
being called together at that period was to take into consideration the Bank Charter Act. They were to pass a
Bill of Indemnity because what had been done with the
Bill of 1844 in 1847 had again been necessary in 1857.
If Government considered the Act of 1844 aggravated the
difficulty in time of pressure, did they mean to continue
that Act while they sought an act of indemnity for neces-

sarily violating it? What! permanently continue an
Act that they knew they must from time to time violate!
He hoped the Government would make up their minds,
and speak out frankly their intention. He hoped they
would not have any more committees to collect evidence
and talk, and decide nothing.

During the debates in the House of Commons,
Mr. Disraeli said :—

It has been in evidence that many men of the highest
authority had given opinions hostile to the Act of 1844,
and it was the duty of the Government on these conflicting opinions to have a distinct and definite judgment.
. . . Were the ministers going to stand by the Act of
1844, or were they not? If they were, he should hesitate
before he agreed to the Bill of Indemnity. . . . He
thought the arguments of the Chancellor of the Exchequer
rested on an unsound basis, for the right honourable gentleman said that the present commercial distress had not
been produced by the currency law, but by the dislocation
of capital and credit. If that were so, why had the Act
of 1844 been violated? (Because the Act had produced
the dislocation.) . . . He thought the House was bound
to come to some definite decision ; and if his amendment
was adopted the House would be placed in an intelligible
situation. His amendment would have the effect of
allowing legislation to go on on this great subject, not to
throw it in a dead lock. . . . He called attention to
three propositions which he considered to be irrefragably
proved. 1. That it was impossible that a banknote, convertible at par, could be depreciated. 2. That no issuer
could press his circulation. And 3. That prices could
not be affected by any circulation of banknotes further
than by an equal amount of metallic currency. He held
that it was proved by the labours of committees of that
House that there was a law affecting banknotes convertible at par, which prevented redundancy or infla-

tion of circulation, and balanced issue and reflux, so as to make them matter of mathematical calculation. . . . It was said the Bank directors were in favour of the existing Act. He had every respect for the opinion of the Bank directors, but would like to refer to the Appendix to the Blue Book already referred to. It was a very entertaining volume (a laugh), notwithstanding its unprepossessing title. The right honourable gentleman then proceeded, in a very humorous strain, to refer to a correspondence between the Chancellor of the Exchequer and the Bank directors, in which they, almost without exception, declared themselves in favour of the Bank Act, attributing the crisis of 1847 to the want of proper knowledge of the principles of banking, but assuring the Chancellor of the Exchequer that they were now so much better acquainted with the subject that a recurrence of the disasters of 1847 was impossible (laughter). It was only after the crisis of 1857 that this was published. He did not know how the Chancellor of the Exchequer could do it (a laugh). He (Mr. Disraeli) could not have done it (renewed laughter). . . . HE WOULD SAY IT HAD BECOME A GREAT NATIONAL OBJECT WHICH STATESMEN OUGHT TO INSIST UPON ACCOMPLISHING, THAT THERE SHOULD BE IN THE BANK OF ENGLAND A GREAT TREASURE AT THE COMMAND OF THE DIRECTORS, WITH WHICH IN MOMENTS OF EMERGENCY IT SHOULD BE IN THEIR POWER TO ASSIST COMMERCIAL DISTRESS, BY INSURING THAT THERE SHOULD BE AN ACTIVE CIRCULATING MEDIUM TO BE EXCHANGED FOR THE REAL PROPERTY OF THE COUNTRY. . . . He was surprised to hear that one of the most eminent men in the country, and himself a peer of Parliament— he referred to Lord Overstone—had declared that, in his opinion, discussion upon this subject was inconvenient and injurious. He (Mr. Disraeli) was surprised that a man so eminent should pronounce an opinion upon the provident privileges of Englishmen. No, the time had come when they ought to arrive at some safe and satisfactory solution of this great question.

Mr. Gladstone said:

The evidence on the subject had accumulated beyond
the possibility of further information being obtained, and
he did not think their ignorance upon what principle the
Government intended the currency to be based was
worthy of the dignity of Parliament. The Bank Act had
failed on two occasions, and it could not stand as it was.
They must look for a continuation of these crises, and he
could not consent that they should be habitually met by a
breach of the law of the land. The Act of 1844, which
was damaged in 1847, was totally shattered in 1857.
Lord Overstone himself had expressed an opinion, that
the time had now come when some elastic provision
should be inserted in the Act of 1844, to meet the
pressure of a commercial panic. This he (Mr. Gladstone)
understood as an avowal of the evils which must arise from
a recurring violation of the law of the land, which left the
power in the hands of the Ministry to decide what houses
should be ruined and what should be saved.

Notwithstanding this strong concurrence of adverse opinion, nothing was done, and we blindly
resumed the policy of regulating our currency by
the foreign exchanges. The old machinery was once
again placed in motion, and in due course we met
with another disaster. Everybody, except Lord Overstone and a few other doctrinaires, agreed in think-
ing that something was wrong, but nobody was
willing to undertake the search for truth, and all
failed to perceive that it lay on the surface of recent
events. The next suspension of this disastrous principle of regulation took place on the 11th May, 1866.
A prolonged and heavy drain of bullion to the East,
in payment of the extra importation of cotton, had

reduced and kept down the banking reserve, and a feeling of distrust had been created by the heavy failures in the East Indian trade which occurred on the termination of the American Civil War, and the consequent heavy fall in the value of cotton, the loss inflicted on this country alone being estimated at 12,000,000*l*. This feeling of distrust was aggravated by those political difficulties on the Continent which resulted in the Prussia-Italian and Austrian War. Things were in this critical condition when the failure of the Contract Corporation, Joint Stock Discount Company, Barned's Banking Company, and several railway contractors under heavy liabilities, took place. A feeling of alarm at once sprung up respecting the new Limited Liability Companies which had been numerously created. This feeling was greatly aggravated by the rapid rise in the rate of discount, and the heavy fall in Stock Exchange securities, more especially in the shares of the new Companies. The fall in the latter was largely increased by the adverse rumours put into circulation and by the heavy and persistent operations for a fall by speculators on the Stock Exchange. The state of affairs was in this critical condition when the Bank rate was put up to 8 per cent. in the middle of the week. This step settled the question. The public was kept in a state of the greatest suspense until the publication of the following weekly return, and a run set in ; and on the failure of Overend, Gurney, and Co., Limited, on the tenth May, it merged into a

complete panic. An unprecedented demand for
assistance arose. The Bank increased its advances
upwards of four millions sterling on the 11th, and
the banking reserve was reduced from 5,727,000*l*. to
3,000,000*l*. in one day. A deputation at once waited
upon the Government, and the restrictive clauses of
the Act were once again suspended. The effect was
immediate on the Stock Exchange, and a feeling of
relief at once prevailed, but credit had been shaken
to its very foundations, and the demand for assistance continued until the end of the month. Between the 9th and 30th May the Bank's advances
upon other securities increased 12,603,246*l*.; the
active circulation, 4,860,510*l*.; the private deposits,
6,951,543*l*.; the total bullion fell 1,277,365*l*.—the
amount held on the 30th being 11,878,775*l*., whilst
the banking reserve on the same day was only
859,980*l*.; the bulk being locked up in the Issue
department in accordance with the great fallacy.

This panic differed in many respects from its
predecessors, but the question at issue is whether the
division of departments aggravated the alarm or not.
There can be no doubt whatever that if the division
had not existed, and the total bullion had been
available, the complete collapse of credit would not
have occurred. The alarm was fostered and aggravated by the action of the Bank in raising the rate
of discount to 7, 8, 9, and 10 per cent. on the 3rd,
8th, 11th, and 12th May, respectively. Such a rapid
rise could not fail to create alarm at any time, but

at a time like this, when so many great centres of credit had been destroyed, it was fatal to every chance of a complete stampede being avoided.

Nothing but a calm and liberal policy could save us from the difficulties with which we were surrounded ; the liberality was forthcoming, but it was neutralised by the extreme rise in the rate. The 10 per cent. rate was prescribed by the Government, and was altogether indefensible. The rate of discount in Paris at the time was only 4 per cent., and as the only export of gold of any consequence which was taking place was to Paris, this extreme rate was not necessary to check it. If it could not be checked by a difference of less than 6 per cent., the attempt to check it should not have been persisted in, and as the subsequent course of events proved, the very raising of the rate to such a ruinous point increased the feeling of distrust on the Continent with respect to our position. The subsequent maintenance of the rate at 10 per cent. for three long months was absolutely ruinous to the industrial and commercial interests. The folly of the policy was proved by the fact that it failed to replenish the reserve, but that no sooner had it been abandoned than the reserve immediately rose, and so continued to rise that at the end of the year the rate had fallen to $3\frac{1}{2}$ per cent., and in the following July to 2 per cent., at which point it remained for twelve months.

It cannot be denied that some of the houses which failed in this crisis were in an unsound con-

G

dition, and this panic has been defended on the ground that it did good by causing their suspension. This argument is as irrational as it is heartless. Panics are not necessary for this purpose. Some of the largest failures on record have taken place when there has been no panic, and when the rate of discount has been far below 10 per cent., and on the other hand many houses rotten to the core have lived through the greatest panics. The heavy failures in the spring of 1865 took place when the rate was at 4 per cent. The Joint Stock Discount Company, the Contract Corporation, Barned's Banking Company, and the railway contractors failed before the panic. The system, which we have seen is based upon such a gross fallacy, is altogether indefensible. A collapse of credit involves in it alike the sound and the unsound, and some of the largest failures which occurred on this occasion were pure misfortunes, and inflicted intense distress and loss.

The most recent instance of the practical working of the system was experienced in the autumn of 1873. The drain of bullion to Germany and the United States, which we had occasion to look into in the preceding chapter, having reduced our central bullion reserve to the extent of a few millions, and the internal currency requirements of the country, and particularly of the Scotch, being at the moment unusually heavy, the banking reserve fell off to a low point, and we found ourselves suddenly plunged into a state of semi-panic. The total amount of bullion held by the Bank was, on the 12th November, 19,338,651*l*., but it was divided by the Act of 1844, and only 8,420,571*l*. of it belonged to the banking department. The remaining 10,918,080*l*. was locked up in the issue department, and could only be liberated and made available by sending in the notes which had been issued against it. These notes were, however, in circulation, and could not at the time be dispensed with, and this is invariably the case whenever a stringency exists, so that in times of our greatest need the gold in this department is virtually locked up. The whole severity of the drain was thus made to fall on the smallest portion of the total reserve. The result was that under the combined drain of gold for export and for home use the directors took measures to protect and replenish the banking reserve, and raised the rate. of discount from 3 per cent. to 9 per cent. between the 25th September and 7th November. This extreme increase within so short a period created the convulsion, and the system exposed us to the danger of all the disaster of a complete panic, which must have occurred if Germany and America had withdrawn a few more millions in gold. And the point is, that it is absolutely certain that if the division in our central bullion reserve had not existed, and the total of 19,338,651*l*. had been available, the extreme rise in the rate of discount and the convulsion and danger would not have arisen.

Other examples of the working of the system

might be pointed out, but the foregoing are sufficient to prove that it is as destructive in practice as it is untenable in theory, and that safety, instead of being found in the maintenance, has been found in the abandonment of the policy. The abandonment invariably dispelled panic and restored confidence, showing that the panics were not produced by the drains, but by that system of regulation the withdrawal of which at once severed the apparent relation of cause and effect between the drains and the panics. The same facts prove that the panics were not produced by speculation or unsound trade, but solely by that system the abandonment of which was invariably found to be the remedy. The system neither prevents speculation nor ensures soundness of trade. It only creates pressure and convulsions whenever it is brought into active operation.

§ 2. The important fact of the existence of the principle of regulation previous to 1844 appears to have escaped attention. The supporters of the system have taken advantage of this, and in answer to the charge that the Act produces pressures and panics, have adduced the fact that they occurred in this country previous to the enactment of the Act of 1844, and occur in other countries where the Act does not exist, and from this they draw the inference that they are not produced by the Act.

In answer to this I contend that it is not the mere Act of 1844 that produces these disasters, but the application of the restrictive principle of regulation on which the Act is founded. This was in operation previous to 1782, was formally adopted by the Court of Directors in 1783, and again in 1827, and was carried into practice on almost the present system in 1840.

The separation of accounts took place in 1840. We had the same distinction in the separation between the issue and the banking department that we have now; we considered that a certain amount was issued against securities, and a certain amount against bullion, and, as a matter of account, that amount was kept as separate as it is under the Act.—*Evidence of the Governor of the Bank of England, given before the Committee of* 1848.

By dividing the Bank of England into two departments, the principle is made to produce its disastrous effects at an earlier stage of the drain, and we had a tremendous panic in May 1866, when the bullion in the Bank stood at 13,000,000*l.*, and in November last we had a semi-panic when the total bullion stood at 19,000,000*l.* Had the Act been in operation in 1825 and 1839, those panics would have been far more intense, and have taken place sooner than they did. If the accounts had been kept on the present plan in 1839, the Bank on the 3rd September would not have had a farthing in the banking department, and the notes would then have been 1,490,000*l.* above the limit. These panics, together with those of 1847, 1857, and 1866, were produced by the operation of the principle of restriction, and were each dispelled by its suspension; in 1825 and 1839 by the action of the Bank under the force of necessity, and in 1847, 1857, and 1866, by the Government suspending it in order to preserve the nation from bankruptcy.

The restrictive system is also acted upon in the United States, Austria, France, and other countries. In France it exists in a modified form only, in the shape of a statutory limitation on the issue of notes, and the limit is fixed at such a high point that practically it is inoperative, the margin between the most extreme currency requirements of the country and the limit being so ample as to prevent any danger of a deficiency arising. We not only place a limit on our issues, but, in conformity to the erroneous assumptions pointed out, also make our currency fluctuate with the foreign exchanges. Neither France nor any other nation besides ourselves does this; and French economists and financiers express the greatest astonishment at our infatuation with such a theory, and at the ignorance which we practically display of the everyday and well-known facts by which its utter unsoundness is clearly demonstrated. French economists and financiers rank amongst the first in the world, and the French monetary system works with greater ease and less friction than that of this or any other country.

Austria also merely places a statutory limitation on the issue of notes, without any reference whatever to the foreign exchanges, but the limit being fixed at too low a point, it constitutes an actual source of danger, and had to be suspended during the recent financial crisis in that country.

The United States not only places a statutory limitation on the issue of notes, but also fixes the proportion of reserve which the National Banks must maintain against the whole of their liabilities ; and consequently their system is almost as wretched as our own. It has been repeatedly suspended in order to save the country from the gravest disasters. It was suspended in 1866, and again during the recent financial crisis. The reserve limit was broken through with the sanction of the Government, and the Treasury came to the assistance of the country by throwing a large amount of currency into circulation in the purchase of bonds and the pre-payment of coupons, and thereby undoubtedly saved trade from the complete dead lock and further disaster with which it was threatened. If they desire to resume specie payments at an early date in the States, nothing is more easy of accomplishment. Instead of trying to screw up the currency to par value by limiting and reducing it, let them set about accumulating a respectable bullion reserve, and they will find that the gold premium will go down as the stock of bullion goes up. As soon as it is sufficiently large they will be in a position to safely decree the return to the cash payments, and then if they consider it necessary they can proceed gradually to call in the notes of small denominations, and replace coin in the channels of circulation. The quantity of notes in circulation at the present moment is not greater than the requirements of the country, and the depreciation cannot rest on a redundancy, for no such redundancy exists, and nothing but the cloud of error which would appear to stick to the Anglo-Saxon race like its shadow stands between the States and the desideratum at which her most eminent statesmen are at the present moment aiming. And the amusing part of the whole thing is this, that in any case, whatever means are adopted for bringing about a resumption of specie payments, the accumulation of a reserve will be an absolute and indispensable condition. Instead of going in for that condition direct, they appear to be inclined to take a circuitous route, and to harass the financial and commercial interests of the country, and of course when at last they do get together a reserve and resume cash payments, the credit will be given, not to the reserve, but to that very manipulation of the currency which shall have covered the country with disaster without really advancing the object in view one iota.

President Grant has just vetoed a bill which had been passed by the Senate and the House of Representatives, the main provisions of which were, 1, fixing the limits of greenbacks and National Bank notes at 400,000,000 dollars each ; and, 2, transferring the reserve at present held against notes and deposits to the deposits only, and requiring it to be kept by each bank in its own vault. The bill would have been an improvement in so far as it pushed into the distance that fertile source of danger, the rigid limit, but it was based upon the old line of error, and was calculated to defer the date of the resumption of specie payments. In such a country as the United States, with its wide-spread and rapidly increasing population, its wonderful activity, enterprise, and prosperity, rigid limits are particularly dangerous, for however ample they may be at the present moment they cannot fail to be reached in a comparatively short time; whilst the country, lulled into a sense of false security, is liable not to discover the fact until awoke to it by the rude shock of panic. The principle is radically wrong. Safety against losses through bank failures should be sought after in a straightforward and sensible manner, and a moment's reflection serves to show that it is by looking to the amount of capital and not in tying up practically unavailable reserves, that it is to be found. The experience of the United States is similar to our own and that of every other commercial country, and it proclaims in letters of disaster that it is absolutely indispensable to the safety of modern finance that careful provision should be made to guard and protect confidence against all disintegrating influences. Over and over again has experience taught that these fair weather arrangements are shattered to atoms by the storm, and that it is futile to tell the world commercial not to be alarmed, that deposits and notes are safe, unless it can be shown that there is a sufficient margin of

cash and available sound credit to meet all effective
demands for discounts and advances. Why cannot
statesmen consent to recognise the vital fact that a
very large proportion of financial transactions are
conducted on credit, and that it is indispensable to
the safety of the whole that this important part be
provided for. This is one of the inner mysteries of
finance, one of the cardinal truths of monetary
science, and demands immediate recognition. Whenever that point has been reached when it became
evident that owing to legislative solicitude or theo-
retical dictum, one part of the financial requirements was being threatened with starvation, panic
invariably set in and imperilled the whole ; and in
every case, in every part of the world, the remedy
has been found in the overthrow of the barrier.
American history teaches this as clearly as our own,
and yet they are blindly adhering to the error. It
is a species of infatuation, but so far from its proving
that we are wiser than our neighbours, it distinctly
shows that we are all, from various motives, rowing
in the same boat, in a frail skiff on a dangerous sea.
It is not the man who is trading within the limit of
his capital or who has a large balance at his credit
with his bankers, that rushes forward to strengthen
his position when distrust is setting in, but those who
are conducting operations on borrowed capital, and
they constitute the bulk of the mercantile community.
Embarked with their capital in large and oftentimes
distant operations, their all is placed in peril by the

breath of distrust, and it is they who go to swell and make up the enormous demand for extra accommodation which feeds the flame of panic. It is in those moments that the priceless advantage of large, powerful, and unfettered banks is seen. Their very presence has again and again proved sufficient. Panic and distrust melt before them like mist before the midday sun. Confidence is the very mainspring of finance, and it is simply folly to decree that it shall not be sustained, a decree which whenever it has been put to the test, has been swept away before the hurricane of panic and confusion which it had created. Dry mathematical dictums have no business in such a matter as this, which is made up of the most sensitive motives of humanity, self-interest and self-preservation; and so long as we adhere to the narrow-minded plan of sacrificing the whole in trying to save a small part, so long shall we find that we are grasping a shadow and losing the substance.

It cannot be too carefully borne in mind that the Act of 1844 is merely a phase in the life of this deplorable error. It simply enforces by legislative means an erroneous policy which the Bank directors had fallen into the error of acting upon, but which it was contended they did not apply with that scientific precision which was, it was said, indispensable to its success. The authors of the Act took for granted that the policy itself was sound, and this constituted the fundamental error on which they proceeded. Had they paused to enquire into the fallacious theory on which they were building, the legislation of 1844, instead of being designed to regulate the currency by the foreign exchanges, regardless of the consequences, would have been designed to support and protect our financial arrangements against the fluctuations in the foreign exchanges and all other disturbing causes. The error consisted not in the method of applying the principle of regulation, as was thought by the legislators of 1844, but in its application at all, and the first step now to be taken is to decide upon the complete and immediate abandonment of this utterly unsound and disastrous policy.

Two great and valuable inferences arise out of the disastrous experience of the past, and it is a matter of supreme importance that they be clearly recognised and carefully borne in mind. They have been purchased at an enormous cost, but are of price-less value. The world advances by successive steps from error to truth, and the rough school of experience is the grand arena in which all valuable knowledge is acquired.

The first of these inferences is that every drain of bullion was fully accounted for by the circumstances of the moment, and clearly arose not out of the imaginary cause assigned by the doctrinaires, but out of the distinct and powerful causes pointed out. Those causes turned the balance of international indebtedness against us, and led to the employment of the international currency, gold. They were well known at the time, were matters of national concern, and stood boldly out from the midst of surrounding events. They lay on the very surface, challenging universal attention, disproving the cardinal error of monetary legislation; and the density of that lamentable infatuation which withstood such convincing proofs of the absolute erroneousness of the fundamental assumption that every drain arose out of an excess and depreciation in our currency, is perfectly astounding and incomprehensible. It is probably the most remarkable instance that has ever transpired of the danger attendant upon a blind devotion to theory. The bulk of its devotees at the present moment have never looked into it, and believe in it because it possesses the merit of being to them an incomprehensible mystery; and we have seen that in one instance at least, Lord Overstone, the latter-day prophet of this strange faith, admitted that he had not submitted it to the test of facts, and did not consider it necessary to do so. What a mountain of misery would have been avoided had he only taken that precaution; what a world of disaster yet unborn may be averted if due attention is at once paid to the lesson taught by experience. Carelessness, utter and wanton, has shielded this evil error from detection, but once more we discover that all is not gold that glitters, that all is not invulnerable steel that for a time successfully resists assault.

The other great and important truth which stands prominently out from the midst of past disasters, and challenges our particular attention, is, that in every instance, without one single exception, the difficulties of the situation were immediately dispelled by the abandonment of the one policy and the adoption of the other. The operation of the one was proving fatal to that confidence on which our financial arrangements rest; the introduction of the other immediately stayed the work of destruction, and rapidly replaced our commerce on its sensitive pedestal. No matter what was the course of events which preceded the difficulty, whether wars, famines, speculation, or legitimate but too rapid an expenditure of capital in railways or foreign loans and enterprises, the one great truth imperatively speaks to us. The circumstances of the time led to an outflow of gold, this led to the active operation of the principle of regulating the currency by the foreign exchanges, and the consequent reduction, or threatened reduction, in the usual facilities of credit. This, striking at confidence, the very foundation of the whole fabric, led to the panic, and that it was the direct producing cause of the panic was demonstrated by the fact that its withdrawal was in every instance immediately followed by the instantaneous cessation of the panic and the restoration of confidence. A clearer case of cause and effect cannot be found in the whole range of reasoning, and that such actually is the true relation between the principle of regulation and panics will be confirmed by a glance at the nature of our financial arrangements.

§ 3. The greatest part of our commerce is conducted on the credit system. Credit is given and received in all the great branches of trade; that is, transfers of capital are made on the condition of payment at a future time. Besides the capital belonging to those engaged in commerce a large supply is thrown into trade by the banking community. Bankers collect capital in innumerable small sums from the whole surface of society, and direct it into the channels of trade by lending it to merchants, manufacturers, and others, and this constitutes the most important part of the banker's business. The greater part of the borrowed capital, and I may safely say the whole of the borrowed circulating capital, employed in trade in this country, passes through the hands of bankers, as the responsible agents between the borrowers and the lenders, and banking is consequently the very centre and support of our commercial system.

Bankers borrow capital on various conditions, but the greatest portion of banking liabilities is payable on demand. The whole of the note liabilities, and by far the greatest part of the deposits, are held on this condition. Millions of capital, nearly all of which is employed in commerce, are thus solely dependent on confidence. It is in the legal power of the real owners of a great part of our trading capital to demand payment at any moment, or by giving a very few days' notice. Bankers, however, from the very nature of their business, calculate upon the maintenance of the confidence placed in them, and make their advances accordingly. Practically, therefore, it is absolutely impossible for bankers to liquidate the whole of their liabilities at any moment. They do not possess the legal power at any moment to call in all their advances on loans or discounts, and if they had the legal power, it would be impossible for their debtors to comply with such a demand. The capital, although principally employed as circulating capital, is nevertheless locked up in trade, and it would take a considerable length of time to complete the operations to which a large portion of it has been directed. Any extensive attempt to do this suddenly would defeat its object, and produce the most disastrous consequences; the very demand would paralyze the credit system and produce a complete collapse of our commercial and financial machinery.

Banking, constituting the centre of the great credit system, should be made as perfect as possible. Previous to 1826, the Legislature prevented the formation of large banking companies, other than the Bank of England, and the country was covered by numbers of small private banking firms. As a consequence, our financial system was in the most unprotected state, and instead of bankers forming a support to credit they were a standing source of weakness and danger.

This piece of legislation was repealed in 1826, when large Joint Stock Banking Companies were permitted to be formed, and at the present time we have the finest and most perfect banking system in the world.

The Bank of England is the grand centre of our credit system. Its reserve of loanable capital is the central reserve of the whole country. Mercantile men place their reserves in the hands of bankers; the country bankers place theirs in the hands of the London bankers and bill-brokers; and these place theirs in the Bank of England. The Bank's reserve is, by this means, the common fund of the country. The reserves of the other section are treated, by that section in whose hands they are placed, as a certain class of deposits, and are to a considerable extent employed, and in that manner the aggregate sum of the reserves is wonderfully diminished, so that the real reserves bear but a very low fractional proportion to the whole nominal reserves. By reserves I mean that class of deposits which is kept at call. The other classes of reserves held by bankers are government securities and cash; the former are generally marketable, but the sale is merely a transfer of cash from the buyer to the seller; the latter class consists chiefly of Bank of England notes, which, in relation to the central reserve, are in precisely the same position as deposits.

H

We thus see the delicate nature of the system on which our gigantic commerce is conducted. The credit system is the means by which the spare capital of one part of the community is turned into the channels of trade, the banking institutions absorbing it on the one hand and lending it out on the other. This capital constitutes a part of the trading capital of the country, hence the necessity of rendering the credit system as perfect and firm as possible. It is evident, from the very nature of the case, that all things which have a tendency to disorganise these arrangements should, if possible, be counteracted and provided against.

The credit system rests upon *confidence*. The term has two significations in relation to this question: first, the trust which men place in each other's honesty and solvency; secondly, the trust which they place in the safety of the system. The latter appears to have been generally overlooked. Unless men had a moral certainty that the credit system was perfectly safe, and of a permanent nature, and believed that they could safely rely upon it for the capital which their extended operations require, they would not place their fortunes in what would otherwise be a fearful vortex. In the majority of cases the capital obtained on credit is indispensable to the borrower's operations: a manufacturer, for instance, who has expended the whole of his own capital in machinery &c., that is, in the fixed capital of his trade, is dependent on credit for his circulating capital, and if this is suddenly cut off, his operations are suspended. Fixed capital is useless without circulating capital, and the capital supplied by the credit system generally constituting the circulating capital of the borrowers, or at least a part of it, the fixed capital of the country is, to a great extent, dependent upon it. The greatest part of that immense fund of capital which is supplied through the credit system has placed the borrowers in a state of dependence, and although in ordinary times they can gradually contract their operations and refund the advances, yet on occasions of sudden and extensive demands this is impossible.

Now, the Bank of England being the centre of the credit system, the confidence in that system depends to a great extent on the ability of the Bank to support credit, and the present system of regulation by, under certain circumstances, threatening to impair this ability, disorganises on these occasions the whole system. The power of the Bank to grant accommodation is restricted, and made to fluctuate with the foreign exchanges. Whenever a drain of gold sets in, and the reserve is reduced to a low point, the system of regulation by forcibly contracting credit, intensifies the pressure and produces panic. Although the Bank may not have contracted its discounts, and the active circulation may not have been diminished in quantity, yet the probability which the regulation creates, that the directors will be shortly compelled to have recourse to those mea sures, gives a shock to the whole system. Commercial men at once attempt to strengthen their position. In ordinary times there exists a large amount of credit afloat, in the form of book debts, and this is now placed upon bills and sent into the banks for discount. The credits are in this manner transferred from the drawers of the bills to the banks, and in its place the drawers create a credit at the banks, and thereby strengthen their position and render their assets more available. Besides this extra demand for discount on the Bank of England, there is another ; the rest of the banking community rediscount at the Bank. In 1857 the Bank's advances on private securities rose from 18,351,990*l.*, at which they stood on the 5th September, to 31,350,717*l.*, by the 25th November ; the private deposits rising during the same period from 9,360,219*l.* to 14,951,516*l.* The system of regulation was suspended on the 12th November.

In 1866 the advances rose 12,603,246*l.* between the 9th and 30th May ; the private deposits 6,951,543*l.*, and the active circulation 4,860,510*l.*

When once in motion, this disorganising operation advances at an increasing velocity. Bankers begin to realise that portion of their reserves which consists of securities ; and this increase in the supply taking place at a time of a decrease in the demand, the prices rapidly decline   The prices also of all those principal articles of commerce which are extensively held on credit, fall, and it becomes impossible to effect sales except at ruinous prices. There is always a large quantity of bills afloat, drawn on the consignees against imports, which are met by the sale of the produce. The state of things rendering a fall in prices probable, there is a rush of holders to sell, but a scarcity of buyers, and the supply far exceeding the demand, prices fall, and commerce is suspended. It is useless to contend against facts ; our credit system is of a most sensitive nature, and vibrates to its very centre the moment the restrictive principle comes into active operation.

The system of regulation also affects confidence, in the ordinary sense of that term. The solvent houses are liable to be involved by the failure of others, and the importance of sound banking institutions is then particularly seen ; the failure of a bank involves in ruin a great number of people who are dependent upon it for support, or who have their reserves in its hands. Consequently, distrust prevails.

This combination of things, which is produced by the restrictive principle, constitutes, when at its height, a panic. High above the whole scene, however, towers a great bulwark of confidence, which even panic, with all its terrible power, cannot impair. Whilst the rest of the commercial world is rapidly succumbing to the hurricane, and houses are suspending one after another, the Bank of England continues to possess the unbounded confidence of the country, and it requires nothing more to allay the storm than an expansion of the credit of that institution. Immediately those floodgates are opened, the commercial vessel once more floats.

The restrictive system, the moment it comes into active operation, acts as a baneful dissolvent upon the very keystone of the whole system—confidence, and our wreck-strewn annals tell the tale of its disastrous effects. No matter what the real cause of the drain, we arbitrarily assume that it arises from the one same sole cause, a depreciated currency, and no sooner does it reach a certain stage than by an act of unutterable folly we let slip the dogs of war, and send distrust and panic stalking through the land, and not until the fair fields of commerce are well strewn with disaster, and wild disorder reigns supreme, do we arrest their march and chain them up again.

Confidence is as indispensable to the existence of our financial system as oxygen is to human life, and the secret of the wonderful success which the anti-restrictive policy possesses lies in the simple but important fact that it restores and revives confidence. It should never be forgotten that confidence is the very soul of all finance; to legislate in ignorance or in indifference to this fact would be to repeat the error made by the legislators of 1844.

Some contend that the vast credit system on which our trade is conducted is perilous, and ought to be reduced to within safer limits. To this there is an unanswerable reply. Let those who think so prove the proposition, and point out a practical remedy. In the meantime let us not continue to increase the danger by imperilling the whole fabric and all the interests dependent thereon by the retention of a system of currency regulation founded upon such egregious errors. In my opinion, and I speak from an extensive practical acquaintance with the subject, our credit system is perfectly safe in itself, and may safely be left in the hands of the parties interested. No doubt grave errors are from time to time made by individuals in the dispensing of credit, but self-interest will do much more, and actually is doing much more, in the direction of limiting those errors to within the closest possible boundaries, than any experimental legislation can do. Our enormous commerce requires commensurate financial arrangements, and England's credit system has done much more towards the building up of that commerce than is generally recognised. Improve it by wise laws as much as possible, but don't attempt to restrict it by any empirical legislation. Prudence is the watchword of all engaged in dispensing credit, and few of us knowingly encourage rash speculation or incur losses intentionally. The system is large, and it is no doubt complicated, but the operations of the country could not be carried on without it. It is surrounded by a thousand safeguards—a perfect army of sentinels are ever on the alert for the advancing foes, misfortune, imprudence, and fraud. Necessity is its *raison d'être*, integrity and confidence its foundations.

The authors and defenders of the Act of
1844 entirely overlooked the important fact that,
not only is it necessary to a sound and perfect
monetary system that the convertibility of the note
should be secured, but that it is of still greater importance that specie payments generally, not only in
respect to the note but in respect to all other financial
obligations also, should be carefully guarded, and
made as secure as possible. It is an error to suppose
that the latter is involved in the former, and that if
we secure the note all the rest is secured. The note
has been to a certain extent secured, but this has
been effected at the risk of the rest of the Bank's
liabilities. In the words of the Lords' Report of
1848, 'It should never be forgotten that the liability
of the Bank consists in its deposits as well as in its
promissory notes. The legal obligation to discharge
both is the same. The failure of either would be
equally fatal. The protection given by the Act of
1844 is usually given to the Bank notes, and in
some degree at the risk of the deposits. This appears undeniable on comparing the reserve, in the
third week of October, with the amount of private
deposits. Had any unfortunate circumstance interfered with the power of meeting the latter engagements, or had not the Treasury letter been written,
there seems little doubt of the fatal consequences
which must have ensued. Had it been impossible
to pay the deposits, a discredit of the Bank note
must have been the consequence, nor can it be

rationally questioned but that such a misfortune might have exposed to risk the convertibility of the Bank notes.'

Looked at superficially the Act would appear to affect the currency only, but on more careful examination it is found to affect the whole fabric of credit on which our vast exchange operations are conducted, and of which paper currency constitutes only a small, although important part; and it is further found that it affects this important fabric of credit in an adverse and mischievous direction. But, strange to say, the Act was expressly designed to do this. Currency was on the one hand regarded as the source of all the evil, and being on the other hand regarded as a powerful lever by which prices could be rapidly and artificially controlled, the Act is intended to bring about a forced fall in prices through a mechanical contraction of the currency whenever a severe drain of gold arises. This contraction shakes the whole credit system to its centre, and has repeatedly resulted in a complete collapse and breakdown of our entire financial machinery. And the absolute necessity of this enquiry into the principle of regulation will be clearly perceived when it is borne in mind that the advocates of the system founded on it regard these disasters as inevitable; they contend that the contraction of the currency is absolutely necessary whenever a drain of gold arises, if we desire to preserve the convertibility of the note, and in the words of G. W. Norman, as reported in

the Commons' Report of 1848—' If, in consequence
of such contractions of issues, inconvenience and
pressure is experienced by borrowers and sellers in
the commercial world, such inconvenience must be
undergone; the inconvenience is an evil, but it seems
to be an evil without a remedy.' Nothing could be
more candid than this, and it is the duty of those
who object to the Act to disprove the theory on
which it is founded and defended. This is what has,
I venture to think, now been done.

§ 4. The forcible application of this utterly unsound
principle of monetary legislation by the Legislature
in 1844, told immediately on the Rate of Discount.
The directors, entering into the spirit of the measure,
at once adopted the policy of making the rate serve
as an auxiliary force to do battle with the foreign
exchanges. They had previously tempered, what
they considered the justice of the policy, with mercy;
but now that Parliament had relieved them of all
responsibility, and placed the policy into mechanical
operation, they loyally determined to lend their
warmest assistance to enforcing it in its entirety.
The result is instructive. Between 1694, when the
Bank was established, and 1844, a period of 150
years, thirty distinct changes were made by the Bank
in its official minimum rate of discount, being at the
rate of one in five years; whereas between the
passing of the Act of 1844, and the 1st January,
1874, a period of not quite thirty years, no less than

218 changes were made in the rate, being an average of seven per annum. This increased fluctuation is at the high rate of thirty-five fold, but large as it is, it fails to indicate the full magnitude of the evil, for during the year 1873 no less than twenty-four changes were made by the directors, being in the ratio of 120 as against every one in the first period, *i.e.* 12,000 per cent. ! !

And not only have the number of oscillations in the rate increased, but the swing of the pendulum has increased also. In the first period of 150 years it was confined within the moderate limits of 3 per cent. on the one side and 6 per cent. on the other ; in the latter period of 30 years it touched 2 per cent. on the one side and 10 per cent. on the other. It might on the face of the matter be supposed that the former period was free from any powerful disturbing causes, but such is not the fact. There were wars, famines, a suspension of cash payments, and tremendous strains upon our national resources, and the nation was shaken to its very foundations by the most powerful convulsions that ever tried the strength of a people. The empire was rent in twain by the American revolution, and the liberties of Europe were imperilled by the ambition of Napoleon, who overran the Continent with his legions, and who would probably have succeeded in his daring enterprise if the gold and blood of England had not been lavished like water to stem the red tide of war and conquest. The balance of international indebtedness was turned strongly against us by all this war expenditure abroad, and panics occurred whenever the restrictive policy was placed into operation. The wealth of the country and the quantity of gold in the world bore a relatively smaller proportion to our operations than they do at the present moment, and yet this enormous disparity has arisen in the fluctuations in the loanable value of money. And if we can only bring ourselves to being satisfied with truth, we shall not have to go far afield to find the cause. It dates precisely from 1844, and is entirely due to the adoption by the directors of the policy of employing the rate as a lever whereby to control the foreign exchanges, and more especially to check withdrawals of gold for export, when, owing to the division of the bullion reserve, the reserve in the banking department is being reduced below what they consider a safe point. In fact they have gradually drifted into looking to the reserve only, and to treating all reductions in the same manner, so that at last there is such an entire absence of all principle of action beyond the mere bare figures, that it is quite impossible to foretell the rate a week ahead; all withdrawals of money, whether from deposits, advances, or discounts; in gold or in notes; for home circulation or for export, being reduced to the same condition of charming simplicity, into a withdrawal pure and simple. Now this would be perfectly disgraceful if applied to the management of a common loan office, but as applied to the centre of the vast financial system of this country it is the height of folly, and is as discreditable to the intelligence of all parties as it is intolerable to the mercantile community. To run up the rate of discount for the purpose of preventing money being withdrawn for the provinces is simply preposterous; it never yet succeeded in that object, and the smallest amount of consideration would suffice to show that it could not possibly do so. When money is wanted to meet the fluctuating requirements of the country, the country bankers can absolutely command it out of the Bank's reserve, whatever the rate of interest may be, and the advancing of the rate, so far from contracting the demand, actually increases it under certain circumstances, by rendering it necessary for the country bankers to largely increase their actual cash reserves as a provision against the feeling of general distrust which the stringent action of the Bank of England creates. The moment the stringency point is reached, the country bankers begin to strengthen their cash balances by calling in their balances from the discount brokers and London bankers, which the latter meet by drawing on their balances deposited with the Bank of England (or by obtaining assistance on discounts), balances which bear no interest, and which the rate of discount in no way protects from withdrawal. The policy is in every respect as short-sighted as it is indefensible, injurious, and dangerous, and the upward movement of the rate is as tem-

porary as it is erroneous. It is an arbitrary interference with the operation of the laws of supply and
demand, and the rebound which those laws bring
about irresistibly carries the rate down again. The
average rate is no higher than it was in the period
preceding 1844, in fact it is lower, but the violent
fluctuations are most injurious and harassing to
industrial and mercantile operations, and infuse a
dangerous speculative element into all engagements
extending over any length of time—a standing
source of danger to all embarked on the sea of
credit. Cheap money is one important factor in
our commercial prosperity, but it would be infinitely
better to have a higher average rate with fewer
fluctuations, than to have these constant fluctuations.
Our complicated commercial interests have a sufficiently large number of disturbing causes to contend
with, without this fresh and artificial disturbing
element, which at one time shatters and withers
commercial enterprise, and throws everything out of
gear, and at another endeavours to resuscitate our
drooping energies into renewed life and activity.
This phase of the principle of monetary legislation
on which we are blindly acting affords a striking
confirmation of Bacon's aphorism, ' Since things alter
for the worse spontaneously, if they be not altered
for the better designedly, what end will there be of
the evil?' We have seen that this evil has been
rapidly altering for the worse ever since its adoption,
and it is high time it was fairly looked into and

abandoned. The policy of monetary legislation which has proved to be of such priceless value in the past, and which I am about to propose to place into complete and permanent operation, will designedly and effectually put an end to this evil and reduce the oscillations in the rate of discount to within their natural limits. The rate of discount is no doubt a powerful lever, but it is a lever which should be employed very sparingly and with great caution. As used at present, it is turned into an intolerable evil, an evil infinitely greater than that which it is employed to counteract. By excessive use it has been converted from being a friendly safeguard into an instrument of disorder. Extremes in this case, as in every other, ought to be carefully avoided, and when a powerful institution like the Bank of England undertakes temporarily to set aside the ordinary operation of the laws of supply and demand, the greatest care should be taken that a balance of good is really ensured. It is not enough to show that an effect has been produced, the question remains, is the result worth the cost? In this case it clearly is not; the greatest instead of the least of two evils is blindly chosen, and we have during the last 30 years been paying a heavy penalty for the error.

It might on the first blush of the matter be supposed that the usury laws accounted for the steadiness of the rate prior to 1844, but such is not the case. The repeal of those laws in 1839 no doubt rendered more extreme rates possible, and would in itself have led to a slight increase in the oscillations, but if the directors had not adopted the policy pointed out, a very small portion only of the increase in the fluctuations would have arisen. I have no doubt some of the defenders of the present state of things will have the temerity to come forward and deny that the directors ever do or can set aside the natural operation of the laws of supply and demand, but any such denial can rest only either on ignorance or on the wilful ignoring of patent facts. The policy of protecting the reserve by advancing the rate is deliberately acted upon by the directors with the entire concurrence and approval of the press and many financial authorities, and it only wanted the vindication of an authority practically acquainted with foreign exchange operations to invest it with an appearance of a scientific improvement in finance. That vindication was forthcoming in Mr. Goschen's work on the ' Theory of the Foreign Exchanges.' But although Mr. Goschen undertakes to be the advocate of this policy, he really confines himself to simply showing that the rate is a powerful instrument. He does not deal with the wider question at issue, as to whether, taking all the facts of the whole question into consideration, it is the *best* policy to pursue. To show that the balance of international indebtedness *can* be temporarily affected by rapid and severe rises in the rate is one thing, to show that the course is under all circumstances advisable is another and altogether different thing. It is only one part of the great question which we are considering, and I venture to think that I shall be able to show that under the policy proposed, these constant and injurious arbitrary fluctuations in the rate will be safely dispensed with, and that instead of violently trying to defer the day of payment of the balances of international indebtedness which from time to time arise, we ought to adopt the wiser and more economical policy of meeting them at once out of our bullion reserve and the constant stream of gold which is flowing hither from every quarter of the globe. It cannot be denied that superficial appearances are in favour of those who, imperfectly acquainted with the subject, contend that the Bank does not interfere with the laws of supply and demand, for like all innovations which have become established, this policy has ceased to look like an arbitrary policy, and the fact that the world outside the Bank parlour often anticipates advances of this description in the rate, lends to the changes the appearance of being brought about by the action of the laws of supply and demand. Let the policy be once abandoned, however, and we shall find that the oscillations in the rate will speedily dwindle down to their old dimensions. It is a mistake too frequently committed to suppose that the laws of supply and demand are never and can never be temporarily interfered with. Because they are sufficiently

powerful to produce fair averages, it is often supposed that artificial extremes are never created, but
the error is confuted by everyday experience.
There is something very agreeable in loftily treating
subjects in a general manner, but it is highly important to the interests of truth and progress that
we should occasionally descend from generals to
particulars, otherwise the enquirer is very liable to
be landed in the region of error. Deliberation is
one of the highest faculties of the human mind, and
when reason sits firmly on her imperial throne, and
the collation of facts is impartial, correct, and complete, the probabilities are that truth will be the
product; but with false scales or false weights truth
is an utter impossibility, error an absolute certainty.
This important subject has been at one time a prey
to the absence of sound reasoning powers, at another
to the presence of erroneous or one-sided facts, and
again and again have the malignant fates brought
about a conjunction of these powerful foes to truth,
and plunged the deluded enquirer into an abyss of
error.

    And not only is the policy of violent and ex-
treme fluctuations in the rate of discount altogether
indefensible on the grounds pointed out, but further,
its success depends upon its supplanting and dis-
placing the powerful corrective force supplied by
the premium commanded by foreign bills when the
exchanges are against us. As pointed out at page
25, this premium tends to restore the equilibrium

in international indebtedness by stimulating exports and discouraging imports, but the raising of the rate, when successful in its object, removes this premium and turns it into a discount. This important fact has been entirely lost sight of by the advocates of this screwing up of the rate policy, and they have accordingly not only committed the error of assuming that it is necessary to take special and severe means to check outflows of gold, but that the raising of the rate of discount is the only sure means of doing this.

Now it must, in the first place, be observed that rises in the rate of discount fail to produce the intended effect when counteracted by corresponding rises abroad, and as a rise here is generally immediately followed by a corresponding rise on the Continent, we find ourselves in an era of competitive rates, in which extreme rates are rapidly becoming more and more common. The responsibility of the creation of this artificial system rests with ourselves, and it is therefore incumbent upon us to set the example of returning to a calmer and more sensible policy. When I speak of extreme and violent fluctuations, it must be clearly understood that I allude not to that class of changes which arises out of the smooth and steady operation of the laws of supply and demand, but to those violent jerks which are made by the directors for the express purpose of influencing the foreign exchanges and protecting the reserve.

When, however, after repeated rises we at last succeed, like those unhappy individuals who find that in the heat of competition they have had knocked down to them the object of their bidding at something like three times what it is really worth, when we at last succeed in establishing a difference of two or three per cent. between the rate of discount here and the rate abroad, the policy effects the transmission of bullion in three distinct ways. If it is not neutralised by panic, as it was in 1866, it (1) causes balances due to foreign creditors to be left here for temporary employment at the higher rate of interest prevailing. (2) It causes the foreign holders of bills upon this country to hold them until maturity, instead of sending them over to be discounted here, and at once withdrawing the proceeds in gold. (3) It causes money to be actually sent over here for temporary employment. In order to produce the latter effect the difference between the rate here and the rates abroad must be sufficiently large to cover the cost of the transmission of bullion, but a much slighter difference will suffice to produce the first and second effects. Now the first and second effects diminish the export of gold, contract the demand for means of remittance, and reduce that premium on foreign bills which was restoring international indebtedness by stimulating exports and restricting imports. The third effect turns the premium into a discount, and positively stimulates imports and contracts exports, and thus not only completely neutralises a powerful correcting force, but inflicts serious injury on the mercantile interest, both through the excessively high rates of discount and violent fluctuations, and through the grave peril to which, under certain circumstances, it exposes our financial system. The policy of making violent and extreme changes in the rate is therefore not only extremely injurious and objectionable, but it is altogether unnecessary, the good it aims at securing being already secured by the harmonious interests of commerce. Before the rise in the rate can turn the exchanges in our favour, and produce an import of gold, not only must the premium here on foreign bills, which was silently but steadily and powerfully correcting our international indebtedness, have disappeared, but it must have given place to a discount. Instead of leaving in operation a counteracting force which would restore the equilibrium in the best and most solid and beneficial manner, we inflict extreme and injurious rates of discount which can only produce an artificial and temporary equilibrium. For as soon as the rate is lowered again the money which has been sent over here for employment is withdrawn, the bills which had been held back are sent forward, and the balances which had been retained are sent on, and the result is that we have paid an extravagant price for the time gained. With twenty millions of bullion at our backs, we imperil the greatest interest of the country in order to command foreign forbearance and assistance, assistance and forbearance which we do not really require. If, however, the time gained enables us to meet the deferred day of settlement with accumulated resources, or allows the balance of 'indebtedness to be discharged by the falling in of foreign credits, the end is held to justify the means, the policy is held to be a complete success, and the perils and disasters to be condoned. But it cannot be too firmly borne in mind that all this screwing up of the rate of discount, with all its evils, leaves the balance of international indebtedness undischarged, and even aims at increasing it, and only secures a few weeks' extension of time. I contend that if we only take a right view of our position, we shall find that we can dispense with this brief interval, and afford to pay our debts as they fall due. We have only to abandon all the deplorable errors of the past, and make up our minds to act rationally in the future, provide a reserve, and *make use of it*, and, *presto*, the difficulties, which appeared so overwhelming, vanish like a dream! It is a pitiable sight to see a miser deliberately refusing himself the ordinary means of happiness, but it is infinitely more so to see a nation of unbounded resources inflicting incalculable injury on its greatest interest out of rank error. It is an invaluable truth, and one which demands recognition at the hands of a commercial people, that the wisest policy to pursue, when the balance of international indebtedness turns against a nation, is to discharge it at once out of the reserve held for the purpose, raise the rate of discount gently and moderately when an unusually powerful disturbing cause has to be dealt with, and then trust calmly to the irresistible correcting laws, and to the elasticity and ever-increasing wealth of the country. For a nation like this, with its annual income of thousands of millions sterling, its annual accumulation of capital of over one hundred millions, its splendid credit and enormous resources, to dislocate its financial machinery whenever a balance of international indebtedness of a few extra millions has to be paid, is a deplorable and warning indication of the confusion and error rampant in this department of human affairs.

CHAPTER III.

PROPOSED PRINCIPLE OF MONETARY LEGISLATION, AND
DEFINITE SUGGESTIONS FOR PLACING IT INTO
-OPERATION.

§ 1. WE have now completed the examination of
the two principles of monetary legislation upon
which this country has been alternately acting during
the whole of the present century; have tested the
soundness of the reasoning on which they are respectively based, and have taken a wide and comprehensive survey of their practical effects. And what
have we discovered? Why, that the favourite principle of the political economists, of the Legislature,
and of a number of the most practical authorities in
the land, is founded on a wonderful mass of error, is
in direct antagonism to the safety of our financial
system, and that whenever brought into active operation it has created difficulties, convulsions, and
disasters; whilst the other, which is in entire harmony with the important, indispensable, and complicated financial machinery by which our vast industrial
and commercial operations are conducted, which is
in complete conformity with the great truths of political economy, and is based alike on sound policy

and common sense, has repeatedly rescued us from the very jaws of destruction into which we were being hurled by its rival. And yet, strange and astounding as the fact is, no sooner have we been saved than we have returned to the very cause of all the evil. Spellbound by the profundity of the errors on which the disastrous system rests, a great nation which, if it can lay claim to any knowledge whatever, might be presumed to understand commercial finance and the elementary laws of political economy, has again and again failed to comprehend the simple truths so clearly taught by its sad experience. We have shown the world the brilliant results of the adoption of the sound economic principle of free trade, but have hitherto failed to work out a sound monetary policy—a failure all the more remarkable from the fact that after having been repeatedly compelled by the force of circumstances to adopt the one and only sound policy possible, we have again and again blindly forsaken it. Anything more remarkable than this, transpiring as it has done in this country of all others, it is impossible to conceive.

It should never be forgotten that the vast industrial and commercial operations of this country are conducted on a complicated system of credit, by which a very large portion of the requisite capital is directed into the channels of production. This capital being absolutely indispensable to the operations grounded upon it, the arrangements by which it is supplied are of the greatest importance to the welfare and prosperity of the country, and ought therefore to be rendered as secure as possible. Instead of drains of gold being made to lead to a contraction of the currency, to undermine the confidence on which our financial arrangements rest, and to interfere injuriously with industrial and commercial operations, they should be rendered as harmless as possible. The termination of all drains being completely secured—1st, by their natural limits; 2nd, by the counteracting forces which have been pointed out, it is no more necessary to legislate for their termination than it is to govern trade by restrictions, monopolies, or bounties.

Instead of rendering a large portion of our central bullion reserve unavailable, as is at present done, we ought to make the whole of it available to meet requirements and to preserve and protect confidence; and instead of violently checking industry and forcibly depressing prices whenever drains arise, we should meet them with a reserve held for the express purpose, and maintain our commerce in as complete a state of activity as possible. Instead of legislating on the model of a purely metallic currency, and for a primitive condition of society, we should legislate for the more advanced and complicated condition of things which actually exists. There is about as much, and no more, reason in aiming at the imitation of the currency arrangements of savages, as there would be in imitating them in their arrangements for their food supply; the former produces intolerable evils, the latter would secure frequent famines. As civilised and rational beings, we ought to aim at the careful avoidance of both results.

In order to place this principle into perfect operation it is necessary, 1. To provide a bullion reserve large enough to meet the utmost probable requirements for our international and home purposes, and also for the maintenance and protection of that confidence on which the whole fabric of financial arrangements rests; and, 2. We must make that reserve available. An ample reserve of bullion is as necessary to the nation as is an ample storage of water to a city, but both should be provided, not simply to be looked at, but for use whenever the necessity arises. Our present policy is as absurd as that of a city would be which, in accordance with some profound theory, locked up its reservoirs, and absolutely prohibited the use of the water except upon impossible conditions, whenever a drought arose. The very essence of the utility of a reserve lies in its being available; to lock it up is to completely ignore the very reason for its maintenance. Vary the conditions on which it may be used by putting up the rate of interest, if necessary, but do not practically prohibit its use, or you at once attack the confidence which it alone can preserve.

The bullion reserve is already provided by our financial arrangements, but we commit the error of rendering a large portion of it practically unavailable. As I have previously pointed out, the Bank of England's reserve is in fact the central reserve of the whole country—the reserve on which all extra-ordinary demands ultimately fall. The Bank holding the spare reserves of the London bankers and discount brokers, reserves placed on deposit and repayable at call, and the Directors knowing from accumulated experience that they are at all times, and particularly in periods of stringency, exposed to an indefinite demand for assistance in the way of advances and discounts, a demand which in time of pressure they could not decline to meet without the risk of causing a withdrawal of deposits, a hoarding of notes, and producing a panic, they have adopted the sound policy of maintaining a large bullion reserve, and will in the future continue to do so. I shall prove further on, that the reserve thus already provided is ample for all requirements.

§ 2. It therefore only remains to make this reserve available, and to place the hitherto temporary policy into permanent operation, and we shall at last be in possession of a sound and secure monetary system.

This can be accomplished by: 1. The *permanent* repeal of the restriction on the Bank of England's issue. 2. The abolition of the division of the Bank returns into the issue and banking accounts, and the amalgamation of the cash reserve. 3. The complete abandonment of the restrictive system of regulating the currency by the foreign exchanges; and 4. The adoption of the policy of protecting and preserving our financial arrangements from derangement, and of supporting and carefully defending the confidence on which those arrangements rest.

These measures would render the reserve fully available, and enable it to efficiently perform the important function for which it is provided, and they would make the Bank of England the great conservator of our monetary system. But as the very essence of this arrangement would depend upon the Directors efficiently and judiciously performing the duties of that position, it is a matter of supreme importance that their hands should be strengthened, and that they expressly abandon the disastrous policy. One important means of securing this would be for the State to place one or two permanent directors on the Bank Board, whose duty it would be to make themselves specially acquainted with the policy, and to keep themselves specially posted up with the condition of trade and the state of the foreign indebtedness of the country, so as to be able to form a sound and correct opinion as to the probable extent and duration of drains of gold whenever they arise. This step would relieve the general directors of a part of the responsibility of the matter, and provide valuable assistance and guidance in all questions of policy, and it would ensure and guarantee public confidence in the administration of the Bank under its enlarged powers.

It is also strongly advisable that the Dead Weight

be converted into consols. This has been repeatedly advised by many eminent authorities, and it would make it into a marketable security.

These measures will render our Central bullion reserve available and of practical utility instead of a large portion of it being locked up in conformity to a profound error, and will enable the Directors to afford that legitimate and indispensable assistance in the future which the repeated abandonment of the restrictive system has enabled them to afford in the past. And they will secure to us the important advantage of the assistance being offered in time to prevent financial derangement arising, instead of being withheld until it has been to a large degree inflicted. Instead of the disasters consequent upon a derangement of our financial machinery being arrested, they will be prevented. So efficacious has the proposed policy proved in the past, and so completely is it in harmony with our financial arrangements, that I have no hesitation whatever in saying that its very presence will effectually prevent alarm from ever arising. It has repeatedly served to dispel panic and restore confidence in the midst of wild disorder, and will efficiently perform the much easier task of maintaining and consolidating that confidence which is the mainspring of the whole system.

§ 3. It cannot be too carefully borne in mind in the consideration of this matter that England is the financial centre of the world, and that the Bank is the financial centre of England. We have seen that a powerful centre of credit is indispensable to the safety of a vast credit system. The country commercial, like the country social, is something more than a mere aggregate of individuals. The latter is a community in the highest sense of the term, bound together by common interests, cemented together by public laws, possessing a central authority vested with ample power to be exercised for the good of the State, and to protect the rights of every individual member from spoliation and danger, and it is absolutely necessary that there should be a similar guardian power in the commercial world. Under the present system there are moments when a few powerful capitalists, by combining to withdraw a few hundred thousands in bullion from the Bank of England, could wreck the commercial interests of the country, and net their thousands by the transaction; and there have been moments when the withdrawal of a small amount through panic has actually produced that fearful result. This is a state of things disgraceful to the intelligence of the country, and when we look back upon the wild assumptions on which it rests, it is perfectly deplorable. The Bank of England has, by the force of circumstances, been elected the central power in finance, but the Directors have failed to recognise the full responsibilities of their position. Instead of guiding their policy by the interests of the country, interests with which their own are bound up, they

have considered it sufficient to mind their own
interest, like the directors of any common loan
office ; and not only have they not consulted the
interests of the country, but they have distinctly
repudiated any such motive, and have stated to the
Parliamentary Committees that they considered that
the Act of 1844 relieved them of all responsibility
outside their own interests, and reduced them to the
position of an ordinary banking establishment. If
the Bank is to retain its privileges, its directors must
distinctly recognize the fact that they are, by virtue
of their position and of our financial arrangements,
entrusted with the guardianship of one of the most
important interests of the nation. The proposed
election of directors by the State will serve constantly
to keep the Board in mind of this fact, and assist
them in acting up to it. The State directors would
be the Financiers-General of the Empire, the Bank
of England their observatory, and the Court of
Directors would carry into effect the conclusions
arrived at from a scientific and comprehensive
survey of the world financial. Instead of interests
of such supreme importance being nobody's business,
they will be the business of the greatest financial
institution of the country, closely linked with the
central authority of the State. Confusion will give
place to order : danger to safety.

The Bank of England may be invested with the
proposed duties with perfect safety. The public
confidence in the ability of the Bank to fulfil all obli-

gations upon which it may enter is unbounded, as
is proved by the fact that even when the Reserve
has stood at a low point, the suspension of the restriction and extension of its issue of notes have been
received with acclamation, and restored confidence
to the mercantile community.   Being the largest
bank in the world, having a capital of 14,553,000*l.*,
and a surplus fund of upwards of three and-a-half
millions; generally holding from twenty to twenty-
five millions sterling of government securities, and
being conducted by directors who are practically
acquainted with our commercial system, the Bank
affords perfect security to the public for its liabilities,
and is especially adapted for being made the great
supporter of public credit.   The restriction was not
imposed on the Bank owing to any doubt as to its
solvency and ability to discharge any of its obligations, but purely and exclusively for the purpose of
making the currency fluctuate with the foreign exchanges, a principle of regulation which, as we have
seen, is based upon a series of profoundly erroneous
assumptions.

The confidence placed in the safety of the Bank
is not only well grounded, but it has been over and
over again expressed by the greatest authorities in
the land.   The following instances on this point will
suffice :—

2494.—Do you mean that with reference to the Act of
1844 your opinion would be that it would be better to
leave the amount of the circulation to the discretion of

the Bank than to attempt to legislate it by an enactment?—I do.—*Evidence of Joshua Bates (partner in
Barings) before Commons' Committee,* 1847–8.

2496.—With regard to the limit which is imposed by
the Act of 1844 you would remove that entirely?—I
should take it away entirely.—*Vide.*

2227.—I don't think it possible to govern a mer-
chant's counting-house or any great monetary institution,
such as the Bank of England, on a rigid rule. You must
place confidence somewhere; you must allow the parties
managing the institution to have a discretionary power.
Sometimes you have an influx of money, sometimes an
efflux; sometimes a bad harvest, sometimes a good one;
sometimes foreign loans, sometimes commercial difficulties
will arise which will make it impossible to govern the
proceedings of the Bank by such a rule as the Act of 1844.

2228.—Then you would leave an institution like the
Bank of England at liberty not only to manage its own
banking concerns at its own discretion, but to regulate
also the currency of the country at its own discretion?—
Yes, I should leave it very much to their own discretion;
but I would not place the Bank in that position that they
should have only their own interest to consult. I would
make them to some extent conservators of public credit.
I would allow them some choice in putting a veto on the
chairman and deputy-chairman, and I would have those
gentlemen possess ample powers, and act under a clear
understanding that they were to consult the public good.
—*Sir William Brown's (Brown, Shipley, & Co.) Evidence before Lords' Committee of* 1848.

5422.—Then you think, upon the whole, that the best
remedy for protecting the public against crises like that
which it has experienced in the past year would be the
entire repeal of the Act of 1844?—Most undoubedly.—
Tooke—Commons' Report, 1847–8.

If I were to offer any suggestion, I should prefer

leaving the whole responsibility of the circulation in the hands of the Bank of England.—*G. C. Glyn—Lords' Report*, 1848.

The majority of the witnesses examined by the Committees of 1847 and 1857 expressed the same confidence in the Bank, and the only obstacle to that confidence being publicly given arose out of the gossamer theory which we have examined. As Mr. Tooke pointed out to the Committee of 1847, the principal advantage to the country which the possession of such a powerful institution as the Bank of England ought to afford ' is precisely that which was taken away from it by the Act of 1844, viz., that upon a general failure of credit there is this vast establishment, with its enormous capital and its unquestioned credit, which can come in and fill the vacuum created by such a general derangement of credit as might otherwise occasion a total suspension of business.' It is not a creation of capital that is required or called for on these occasions, but the maintenance of confidence in our financial machinery through the extension of the best and most effective form of credit.

§ 4. With respect to the question which here naturally presents itself, what amount would constitute an ample bullion reserve, I am of opinion that an average of 20,000,000*l.* would do so.

Taking the period between the 1st January 1870 and 31st December 1873, a period during which powerful disturbing causes were in operation, and during which violent fluctuations in the reserve took place, it will be found that the lowest point to which the bullion in the Bank fell was 18,761,616*l.* at which it stood on the 4th August, 1870, when the rate of discount was raised from 5 per cent. to 6 per cent. ; and the highest point ever reached was 27,444,441*l.* on the 27th July, 1871, when the rate was at 2 per cent. The average for the whole period was 22,000,000*l.* The fluctuations would, no doubt, have been slightly greater had not the rate of discount been violently and repeatedly raised for the purpose of checking the drains, but if we allow the ample amount of 1,761,616*l.* as having been thus retained, this would only reduce the lowest point touched to 17,000,000*l.*

It is a remarkable and reassuring fact, that the most severe and prolonged drain which has occurred did not reduce our central bullion reserve by a greater amount than 7,623,000*l.* Taking the reduction between the raising of the rate of discount from the lowest immediate preceding point to the highest point reached during the drains, I find that the results are as follows :—

Between March 1795, when the rate was at 4 per cent., and 25th February 1797, the date of the suspension of cash payments, the bullion fell from 7,940,000*l.* to 1,272,000*l.*, a reduction of 6,668,000*l.*

Between April 1839, when the rate stood at 3¾ per cent., and the 15th October, when it was at

6 per cent., the bullion fell from 7,073,000*l.* to 2,525,000*l.*, a reduction of 4,548,000*l.*

Between 17th August 1846, when the rate stood at 3 per cent., and 25th October 1847, when it stood at 8 per cent., the bullion fell from 15,935,000*l.* to 8,312,000*l.*; a reduction of 7,623,000*l.*, the greatest reduction ever experienced.

Between 26th June 1856, when the rate stood at 4½ per cent., and the 20th November 1857, when it stood at 10 per cent., the bullion fell from 13,073,758*l.*, to 6,484,096*l.*, a reduction of 6,589,662*l.*

Between 15th June 1865, when the rate stood at 3 per cent. and the bullion at 16,045,669*l.*, and the 30th May 1866, when the rate stood at 10 per cent. and the bullion at 11,578,775*l.*, the reduction was 4,166,894*l.*; and

Between the 21st August 1873, when the rate stood at 3 per cent. and the bullion at 24,185,320*l.*, and the 8th November 1873, when the rate stood at 9 per cent. and the bullion at 19,338,651*l.*, the reduction was 4,846,669*l.*

It follows from the foregoing facts: (1), that the Reserve can in ordinary times be kept up to about 20,000,000*l.*; (2), that judging from the experience of the past, and allowing for much greater disturbing causes in the future, an average bullion reserve of that amount would be ample to meet all demands for export, and at the same time protect us against a shock to credit arising from any danger of the complete exhaustion of the reserve. The experience of the past is a safe guide in the matter, and justifies us in laying down the proposition, that with an average bullion reserve of 20,000,000*l.* we can safely face the most prolonged and heavy drain that is ever likely to arise.

There is usually an annual excess of between four and five millions sterling in the imports of gold over the exports, and it would be very much greater were it not that we annually invest large sums in foreign securities. The total import of gold in 1872 was 18,337,852*l.*, and in 1873 20,462,015*l.* The total imports of gold and silver during the same periods amounted to 29,505,319*l.* and 33,454,724*l.*, respectively, the average monthly import during 1873 being 2,787,893*l.* With this powerful bullion current, what absolute folly it is to act as at present whenever the balance of international indebtedness turns a little more than usual against us. What we ought to do should be to firmly confront the fact, apply the incoming stream to satisfying the demand, and, if necessary, dip without hesitation into our central reserve. A very brief and even partial intermission in the export would soon suffice to re-plenish and reconstruct it.

If at any time in the future this provision should prove to be insufficient, they must fall back upon the large amount of gold in the channels of circulation, estimated to amount to about 75,000,000*l.*, or upon the expedient of opening credits on the Continent, two very powerful and unobjectionable means of meeting extraordinary emergencies. The first can be done by the partial displacement and absorption of the coin in circulation by the temporary issue of 1*l*. notes; the second, either by the Bank arranging for an open credit itself, and throwing the bills drawn against it on to the market, and thereby supplying the demand for remittance, or by arranging with the Foreign Exchange dealers to do this, as was done in 1839. No stone should in any such event be left unturned, and no expedient neglected, to assist the country over a temporary difficulty, and to prevent a derangement and breakdown in our financial machinery. If such a disaster should at any future time be absolutely inevitable, it should not be allowed to take place until every means to prevent it had been completely exhausted.

When I say that I consider that an average of 20,000,000*l*. should be aimed at, it must be understood that I do not propose that the directors should take violent measures to keep it at about that point, at one time lowering the rate outrageously in order to employ the surplus, and at another screwing it up to protect it. All arbitrary fluctuations in the rate are objectionable on precisely the same grounds as constant chopping and changing in the system of taxation is objectionable; the one disturbs the incidence of taxation after things have adjusted themselves to it, the other disturbs one of the factors which enter into prices, contracts, and commercial transactions. Whilst aiming at providing about twenty millions, yet when temporary and comparatively slight disturbing causes arise and affect the balance of international indebtedness, the reduction in the reserve should be viewed with calmness, and arbitrary changes in the rate should be carefully avoided; for as it is absolutely certain that all drains are limited in extent, we may in all such cases safely leave the rate in the hands of the ordinary laws of supply and demand, confident that as soon as the balance has been paid the reservoir will be speedily refilled by the bullion stream which is constantly flowing into our coffers. We may safely fall back upon the reserve without alarm; it is provided for that purpose, and should be employed fairly and freely, without the imposition of any unnecessary conditions.

There exists a singular tendency, even in the minds of those practically acquainted with finance, to regard this central bullion reserve as something sacred, which should never, under any circumstances whatever, be permitted to dwindle down below a certain point. As this idea is absolutely fatal to the very essence of the utility of a reserve, it will be as well to point out its fallaciousness.

As a matter of fact reserves, whether of gold, corn, iron, cotton, or any other article, ought to be provided and accumulated in ordinary times for the express purpose of being fallen back upon and made use of when the contingency against which they are

provided arises. And practically such is the case, for
the restrictions to the contrary have, as we have
seen, been invariably swept away whenever put to
the test. The fallacy springs out of the fear that
the application of the reserve to its only use
would expose us to the risk of being some day
left face to face with an empty exchequer. And
undoubtedly it would do so, but so likewise
would the use, between the seasons of production,
of corn, wine, and other products of the earth.
Looked fairly in the face, the question turns out to
be one of probabilities, and so long as we provide
against the most remote probability of utter exhaustion, and advance, as it is in this matter proposed to
do, a considerable distance into the region of improbabilities, then these idle fears may be safely
abandoned. The maintenance of an average reserve
of twenty millions will fully protect us from any
such danger, the probabilities being that it would
never be necessary to entrench upon it to a greater
extent than one-half—probabilities based upon a
wide field of experience, and a careful survey of the
whole of the facts of the matter. But even if misfortune on misfortune piled did ever threaten to
sweep away the whole of this solid rock of gold,
yet it would be infinitely more rational to be satisfied
with one such disaster rather than as at present
continue to artificially create many, by artificially
placing the country in the position of having no
available reserve by locking up and rendering the

actual reserve unavailable. If we are to perish let us at all events live as long as possible and die rationally. As long as there is a copper in the reserve with which to tide over the difficulties of the moment, so long should we bravely face the adverse storm, and when the last is done, or rather some time before that, we should gallantly bring up our reserve forces, the coin in the channels of circulation and our splendid credit. What would be thought of any man who, on the grounds that another dearth might succeed the present one, was to propose that the Indian Government should lock up the present store of rice which has been got together for the support of the famine-stricken population of vast districts of India? If any man were to come forward with such a flimsy argument, and gravely advocate that the population should be left to perish rather than that the food reserve should be used,—that it should only be given up in exchange for the life blood, as the gold in the issue department can only be given up for the notes, the glaring folly of the proposal would be clearly seen, and yet that is a strictly parallel case to the views generally current respecting the central bullion reserve of this country. When will childish timidity give place to reason, and when will the world practically act up to the truth that reserves are accumulated in periods of plenty for use and not for ornament in the day of threatening calamity? It is a duty to prepare for adversity, but where is the use of prudence if folly is allowed to step in, and, locking up the reserve out of fear of magnified possibilities, overwhelm us with all the very evils against which we had so carefully provided? The nervous timidity which would lead a general to hesitate to call up. his reserves at the critical moment to stave off defeat and to win victory; which would induce a statesman to preserve the food and sacrifice the lives of the famishing people; which would make the commander abandon his ship on the first approach of the storm, instead of sticking to her until every means for her preservation had been completely exhausted—these and other similar glaring exhibitions of folly and cowardice would amount to a crime, and subject the perpetrator to punishment accordingly; and yet we deliberately throw away the brave ship of Commerce long before the point of real danger has been encountered. It is out of such a miserable species of folly that we lock up our central bullion reserve, and scatter ruin and disaster around, because forsooth if the improbable was to occur disaster would be inevitable. What we have to do as rational beings is to provide against the reasonable probabilities of life, and taking care to have a good margin beyond that, confidently use our reserves when the necessity for doing so arises.

There is another point closely connected with this question of reserves, which I will here notice. It is the too exclusive attention paid to the reserve by the Directors in their regulation of the rate of

discount. In the cotton, corn, iron, and other
markets, the stock in hand is only one of the many
causes which go to determine prices. The state of
trade, the demand, the supply, the state of prices
abroad, and all the numerous elements which
make up what is termed the supply and demand,
immediate and future, are taken into consideration,
and ought to be done with respect to the loanable
value of money. In the general market it takes a
powerful cause indeed to double the price of any
article, but the loanable value of money is run up,
and doubled and trebled on the most insignificant
grounds. And yet when the point comes to be
fairly looked into, and foregone conclusions and pre-
conceived ideas are thrown aside, it becomes evident
that there is no real ground for this wide disparity.
The average rate of interest in any country depends upon the degree of general safety insured by
the form of government, the state of public credit,
the relation between the accumulation of capital
and the demand for it, the state of commercial
morality and the general degree of safety under
which financial transactions can be conducted, and a
variety of other conditions; and there really is no
reason why the extent of the oscillations of the rate
around the mean point should exceed in degree the
corresponding oscillations in the intrinsic value of
gold, corn, &c., &c., around their average value.
There may be reasons why the fluctuations should
be more frequent, but there are none why they

should be more severe. When money is flowing
out of the Bank into the country to satisfy a
periodical and temporary demand, the nature of the
outflow should be allowed its full weight. When,
again, it is being taken for export, the nature and
probable extent of the drain, together with the
known and probable supplies coming forward, should
be. taken into account, and instead of fluctuations
pure and simple in the amount of the reserve, or in
its proportion to the liabilities, constituting the sole
test, it ought to constitute a small part only. It is
not enough to be satisfied with the effects only; the
causes in operation should be allowed their place in
the question, and until this is done it will be
hopeless to look for an intelligent policy. It is also
of importance to observe that although the loanable
value of money would be determined by the laws of
supply and demand if the market was perfectly
open, and left to adjust itself free from all pre-
conceived ideas, yet it must be borne in mind that
fluctuations are not necessary in this case, as they
are in that of corn and other articles. It is quite
necessary that the price of corn should fluctuate, for
the purpose of partially regulating the consumption,
but this is not applicable to money. If there is too
great a demand or supply of capital at any time, it
will find its adjustment through the prices of
commodities and values most in request, and it is
not in the slightest degree necessary that the rate of
interest be brought to bear upon the matter, and

the idea to the contrary, like so many other errors, arises out of a one-sided view of the fact having been taken, for nothing are more delusive than half-truths and one-sided facts. Whilst a permanent advance of the rate of discount to a high point would reduce the demand for money and for capital, by crippling commercial and industrial enterprise, temporary fluctuations have frequently the opposite effect. The advance in the rate may possibly be shown to curtail the demand in one direction ; but the point to be looked at is whether on the balance it does so, and experience has again and again demonstrated that it does not. Variations in the internal demand for money simply indicate variations in the extent and activity in the exchange of values, and in the extent to which money is being used as an instrument of exchange, and it is to the price of commodities, and not to the loanable value of money, that we have to look for the proper adjustment of exchange operations. Restrictions on the quantity of the instrument, currency, and artificial fluctuations in its loanable value, are as unnecessary as they are injurious and dangerous.

There is one error connected with this part of the subject, which it will, perhaps, be as well to notice and dispose of. I allude to the assertion, frequently advanced, that the stock of bullion now maintained by the Bank is due entirely to the Act of 1844, and that if the restrictive clauses of that measure are abandoned, the reserve will immediately dwindle down to its old dimensions.   It is apparent, on a little reflection, that this opinion is ill-founded. The extent of trade, the enormous increase in the stock of precious metals in the world, and the condition of things generally are altogether different to what they were prior to 1844, and the directors will possess precisely the same means of maintaining the reserve at the elected average point after the proposed changes as they do at the present moment, and it will be the duty of the State directors to see that they do so.   This is one of the conditions on which the Bank should be confirmed in its privileges— privileges which entail responsibility and duty to the country as well as advantages to the proprietors. This duty was not clearly recognised by the directors prior to 1844, but it is well known that, although they now disclaim it, they really act upon it as a necessity imposed upon them by their position as the custodians of the central reserve, and they will have no hesitation in fully agreeing to recognise it as a duty in the future.   Sir Robert Peel, Mr. Disraeli, Mr. Tooke, and other eminent authorities saw the value of such an arrangement, and pronounced in favour of it, but what is now accomplished with ease was then regarded as difficult of attainment. ' I think,' said Mr. Tooke, ' if instead of this most unfortunate Act of 1844, there had been an arrangement made with the Bank, that the directors should consider themselves bound to maintain an average amount of treasure, double at least of that which

they had maintained in the ten years prior to the
renewal of the charter, namely from 1833, we should
have avoided a good deal of the inconvenience connected with the management of the Bank. We
should not have had either the difficulties of 1836
and 1837, or of 1839, if in each case the drain had
begun with an amount of treasure such as in 1846,
and there need not in that case have been the
slightest attention paid to the circumstances of the
drains for foreign payment which occurred at
those periods.' This sound authority pointed out
that the reserve was undergoing a natural process
of increase, that during the ten years from 1833
to 1842 the bullion in the Bank was only about
6,800,000*l.* ; but that on March 23, 1844, before the
passing of the Act, and before it was known what
the new arrangement was to be, it had risen to
16,395,000*l.*, an amount which exceeded the average
balance held under the Act during the following
twenty years. Mr. Tooke told the Committee of
1847, that he thought an average balance · of
12,000,000*l.* would be ample for the Bank to aim at
maintaining. With our largely increased commerce
it will be advisable to exceed that figure ; the interests
at stake are now so much greater that it will be only
a matter of common prudence to aim at keeping an
average of 20,000,000*l.* There will be no difficulty
in doing this ; the difficulty which then existed has
now been solved by the largely increased gold production of the last twenty-five years, and by the

command which our increased commerce and wealth give us over nearly the entire gold production of the world.

The defenders of the Act have claimed for it the credit of at all events locking up a store of bullion in the issue department which we have thrice been able to fall back upon by the suspension of the Act, and they have not hesitated to claim this as a great advantage secured by the Act, and to maintain that had it not been for the Act, there would have been no such store in existence. The audacity of this statement is only exceeded by its utter erroneousness. As a matter of fact, pressures and panics are absolutely antedated by the Act, and brought about when but for this division of departments they would not occur. In dividing our store of treasure we act like the miser, who, gloating over the heap of treasure, refuses sustenance to his frame, and sinks into the grave feasting his eyes on his heap of gold. After blasted prospects, ruined fortunes, and wide-spread disaster are heaped like a sacrifice on the altar of error, we repeal the restriction, and with a single touch of the magic wand of confidence, restore life to the withered frame of our commerce, and then exclaim, See the wonders of economic science! The very breakdown of the system based upon error is audaciously appealed to in its defence. Could anything more preposterous or deplorable be conceived? And yet the argument is used in perfect good faith. The advocates of the system really be-

L

lieve that disasters are inevitable, and are produced not by their system, but in spite of it. And from their point of view the opinion appears to them to be perfectly sound. It is quite consistent with, and logically follows the central assumption upon which the system is built. If that assumption is true, if a contraction of the currency is absolutely necessary to stop outflows of gold, then it would undoubtedly be infinitely better that the remedy should be called in at an early stage of the drains, rather than at the last moment only, and it was because he believed it to be true that Lord Overstone, in his reply to the petition of the London merchants, in 1847, declared that it was necessary that the power of giving temporary aid, if called for by the mercantile body in periods of emergency, should NOT exist. But we have seen that the assumption is as false as false can be, and that it is altogether an unfortunate blunder.

The practical and absolute evil of this system of antedating panics was signally illustrated in 1847. The outflow of gold on that occasion, which had been produced by the extra importation of corn, ceased about the end of April, and from that date to the end of the disastrous month of October, the foreign exchanges were continuously favourable to this country, and no outflow was taking place. And yet mark what happened. The flame of distrust which had been created by the operation of the Act in April, and which had been almost fanned into the lurid flame of panic by the action of the Bank of England in cutting down the ordinary facilities of discount to the principal banks and centres of credit in the country, had shaken our financial arrangements to their foundation, and produced a chronic feeling of dread and caution on the part of all embarked on the sea of credit; so that when the usual quarterly drafts of the imperial exchequer began to play on a weak banking reserve—a reserve which the famine and its effects had prevented from being speedily replenished, the flame of distrust once again broke forth, and the sleeping volcano burst into fearful and destructive activity. The foreign exchanges were favourable and had been so for months before, and even according to this erroneous theory there was no reason why the 9,000,000l. of treasure in the issue department should be locked up and rendered as unavailable for all practical purposes as if it had been buried in the wilds of Siberia. And yet the defenders of the Act claimed credit for having both created and preserved this store of bullion. Is it not clear that this claim is unfounded? In the first place the store had been created prior to the passing of the Act; in the second there was no external drain threatening its exhaustion, and altogether the great evils of the panic were inflicted upon the country unnecessarily. If the Act had been suspended before the distrust set in, the panic would not have occurred. The system was the cause, and the policy on which the system is based had in-

variably been the cause before the passing of the
Act, and distrust and panic were the result.   If the
Act had been suspended before this panic arose the
store of bullion would have been precisely as much
our own property and as safe against this imaginary
tendency to run away, as it was after the eventual
suspension of the Act, with, however, this important
difference, it would have served the higher purpose
of maintaining confidence instead of restoring it ; it
would have protected us against all the evils of panic
instead of rescuing us from the gulf of disaster.   The
credit claimed for the Act is altogether groundless,
and it is really astounding how it can have been
put forward in face of the facts by which it is so
completely demolished.

Two distinct and opposite, but alike fatal errors
have been committed in the past with respect to the
bullion reserve.   Prior to 1844 there was the error
of not providing a sufficient reserve.   Since it has
been provided ; but a large portion has practically
been rendered unavailable until the effects of the
division swept away the barrier.   Common sense,
like truth, lies between extremes, and dictates in this
case that a reserve both ample and available be
provided.

§ 5.   The unfortunate results of this fatal error do
not however end here.   When the Governments of
1847, 1857, and 1866 were compelled by the
force of overpowering circumstances to suspend the

restrictive clauses of the Act, to break the law in order to prevent its breaking the Bank and ruining the country, they attached to the suspension the condition that a high rate of discount should be charged. During the debate in 1847 Earl Russell stated that this was done for the purpose of preventing the liberated treasure from running away, and the 8 per cent. rate imposed in 1847, the 10 per cent. rate in 1857 and 1866, and the still higher rate of 12 per cent. which Mr. Lowe attached to his extraordinary proposals, were no doubt all based upon the same ground. Need I point out that this ruinous precaution rests on the unfortunate fallacy which underlies the whole matter, the erroneous assumption that all drains of gold arise from a depreciation of our currency, and that the high rate was intended to serve as a substitute for the suspended restrictive principle? It appears perfectly incredible that such an opinion could be for one moment seriously entertained by practical statesmen, but so is the whole thing likewise incredible, and this very incredibility has hitherto proved its strongest defence. If the drain did really arise from a depreciation in the *intrinsic* value of gold, it would be difficult to conceive how a rise in the *loanable* value of money could correct it, and it is capable of demonstration that it could have done no such thing, and the imposition of the high rate was only placing a smaller error in the room of an infinitely larger one. It was better to

have the money and the succeeding confidence at
10, 12, or even 20 per cent. than not to have it at
all, but it would have been still better to have had
it free from so unnecessary a condition, a condition
so ruinous to the mercantile interest. The mere
permission to use the reserve answered the purpose ;
it restored confidence, and removed the cause which
had excited the want, but the action of the Governments empowered the banking interest to levy black
mail upon commerce, a levy injurious to the true
interests of both parties, as it laid the seeds of future
losses to the bankers, both in the impoverishment of
their customers, and in the strangling of commercial
enterprise. The evils inflicted by the system do
not all come to the surface during the convulsions,
the future cause of ruin is planted in many a house
which, robbed of its capital by the disasters through
which it has barely managed to pass, struggles on, it
may be for many a year, maintaining an uphill fight
against the difficulties which such losses entail.
And the dislocation in commercial connections and
in industrial operations throughout their multifarious
ramifications in every quarter of the globe, paralyzes
and checks international exchanges, and, as in 1866,
leads to a stagnation in trade extending over several
years. The infliction of high rates by the Government was altogether erroneous. If the object aimed
at was to control the foreign exchanges, all that was
required to attain that object was a rate slightly
above the rates abroad, and it should have been left

to the judgment of the directors to determine what that rate should be. The proposal to impose the uniform rate of 12 per cent. in every instance, entirely irrespective of the actual rates ruling abroad for the time being, was carrying the error to its extreme limits, and it certainly astonished the commercial world. When we reflect upon the important fact that a ruinous rate so enforced by the State is inflicted on the whole mass of commercial transactions entered upon or renewed during the period, and that the proportion in which it falls on discounts for gold export purposes, in comparison with its incidence on home transactions, is absolutely infinitesimal, the atrocity of the policy is self-evident, and it becomes clearly apparent that of two evils we choose the greatest. If there is a balance of a few millions to pay, pay it and have done with it; don't ruin the greatest interests of the country in order to defer the day of payment. We are the bankers of the world, the owners and lenders of such enormous masses of capital as the ancient empires never dreamt of. We lend to the world by millions at a time, annually accumulate by tens of millions, and yet when we happen to have invested rather closely, or when one or two of our great financiers have entered into engagements in respect to foreign loans, engagements which they have the power of carrying out whatever the rate of discount may be : whenever the balance of international indebtedness is for the moment turned against us by any of the innumerable causes and accidents, and we have to fall back upon our reserve to the extent of a million or two more than usual, we go off into convulsions as if we were on the verge of bankruptcy.

§ 6. There are two remarkable circumstances connected with the discussion of this question with which I have been much struck. 1st. The almost complete avoidance by the combatants of the consideration of the fundamental assumptions upon which the whole system is built; and 2ndly. The constant and persistent appeal to the authority of Sir Robert Peel in defence of the system.

These wonderful assumptions appear to have been respected from a feeling of awe created by the absolute impossibility of comprehending them as truths, and the idea of subjecting them to the test of facts seldom appears to have suggested itself. The moment this is done they dissolve into thin air like the baseless fabric of a vision, and their profundity is found to consist not in profound truth but in gross error.

With respect to the defence grounded upon the authority of Sir Robert Peel, it cannot be rebuked more sternly than by the words of that great statesman himself. During the debate on the Act on 30th November, 1847, he said : ' The subject is plainly open to reconsideration. That it would be absurd for anyone to claim identity of opinion now with any opinion he might have expressed in 1844,

I freely admit. I think nothing could be more injurious to the country than that any man should now refuse to come to a different conclusion to what he did in 1844, after the experience of the intervening period, or even the consideration of the question, on the ground that the House had already had all this information. I think it would be perfectly justifiable for the House, if they should see reason for doing so, to adopt a different line, but I think it would be hardly justifiable for the House of Commons to say, " We gave our consent blindly and inconsiderately to the measure proposed to us by the minister." ' The latter sentence is in allusion to a remark of Mr. T. Baring's, that he and others had voted in favour of the Bill in 1844 from confidence in those who proposed it, and as an experiment.

Now, Sir Robert Peel pointed out in the course of this debate that Committee after Committee had sat and talked and taken evidence on the subject, and that in 1841 the questions put to the witnesses amounted to 14,000, without any practical resolution having been arrived at. He therefore thought that enquiry on the subject had been exhausted, and that the best course was to propose some definite measure and invite the House to come to some practical conclusion. No one knew better than did Sir Robert Peel the utter confusion of ideas which prevailed about the matter ; and it is no secret that his own opinion respecting the Act of 1844 underwent a considerable change, and that he did not by any means regard it as a final measure. He continued to defend those clauses of the Act which dealt with the provincial issues, and the reasons on which that defence was based were undoubtedly good and well grounded. It is a mistake to suppose that every particle of the Act is indefensible. In so far as it put a stop to the extension of the issue of notes by weak and insecure issuers, it was decidedly a step in the right direction, and in respect to these issues it was evidently the object of the Legislature to protect the public from loss through the failure of the issuers on the one hand, and to make the circulation fluctuate with the foreign exchanges on the other. With respect to the issues of the Bank of England, however, the intention of the Legislature was purely to make them fluctuate with the foreign exchanges. The Act was a composite measure, based, or rather defended on a variety of grounds, many of which are sound. Sir Robert Peel defended the measure, after its failure in 1847, by showing that the evils and losses which had repeatedly arisen through the failure of small country issuers before the passing of the Act had been to a great extent put a stop to. The Act, by prohibiting the further formation of small banks of issue, undoubtedly conferred a great benefit upon the country, for this had been the source of very heavy losses to the public and of internal weakness to our financial arrangements. He, however, made no attempt to deal with the fundamental error, that of regulating the currency by the foreign exchanges. This was unfortunately allowed to pass unchallenged by all parties, it being erroneously regarded as a sound but abstruse proposition, which had been satisfactorily and completely established by the political economists.

Even the Committee of the House of Lords which condemned the Act of 1844 did not detect this fundamental error. It reported in favour of a suspensory clause being added to the Act, to be exercised, however, only when the foreign exchanges were favourable. The Bullion Committee of 1810, and the late Government, attached the same condition to their proposal, and the reason in the three cases was evidently the same, the supposition that the Act was based upon sound principles, and that the forcible contraction of the currency was necessary so long as the foreign exchanges continued adverse, a supposition which we have clearly seen to be altogether erroneous.

§ 7. The proposed measures will completely reverse our policy of currency regulation, and place into operation the hitherto invariably successful but neglected principle; and not only will the convertibility of the note be secured, but the principle of specie payments generally, not as at present in respect to the note only, but in respect to all other obligations also, will be placed on sound and secure foundations. The English Provincial, the Scotch and the Irish issues remain to be dealt with, but on this point it is not necessary to do more than indicate the outline, without attempting to enter into an elaborate examination of all the *pros* and *cons* of the matter.

As has been already pointed out, the Acts of 1844 and 1845, in aiming at making the currency fluctuate with the foreign exchanges produced one decidedly good effect, they prevented the further growth of small unsafe issuing bodies, and were in this respect a step in the right direction, but the same cannot be said with regard to the blow which was aimed at the maintenance of a plurality of issuers. The concentration of the power of issuing would no doubt have its advantages, the chief of which would lie in the uniformity of the note, and in its free circulation in every part of the kingdom; but it would have its drawbacks also, and the latter would, in my opinion, overwhelm the former. By throwing the whole of the fluctuations in the currency requirements of the country on to one point instead of distributing them over a large surface, it would constitute a powerful disturbing cause in the money market, an effect partially felt under the present stage of advance in that direction. What we have to aim at is the creation of a just system of a plurality of safe issuing bodies. The only duty of the State in the matter is to see to the general safety of this particular form of credit; safety, not against any imaginary danger, but against loss to the note holder through the failure of the issuers. The object to be aimed at in respect to these issues, is (1) To apply to them the general principles of monetary legislation pointed out. And (2) to place them on a safe and just basis. The first necessitates the removal of the present rigid and narrow limits ; the second involves the throwing open the right to issue notes, subject to such conditions as shall secure to the public every reasonable degree of safety. If we are contented to deal fairly with the vested interest which the law has created, and to mete out equal justice to all at present outside the pale of issue, there will be very little practical difficulty in disposing of the matter in a satisfactory manner.

Taking the English Provincial issues first, their present position is this : The authorised limit at the present time is 6,653,966*l.*, of which 3,915,326*l.* belongs to 118 private banks, and 2,738,640*l.* to fifty-six joint stock banks. This limit is perfectly rigid, the English provincial issuers not being allowed the privilege granted to the Bank of England and the Scotch and Irish issuers, of issuing notes against the gold in hand.

The limit of issue of the 118 private banks ranges from 3,201*l.* up to 130,757*l.*, the average being 33,000*l.* only ; an amount so insignificant that it is evidently unnecessary to disturb the arrangement on the grounds of safety. The private bankers of England are at the present moment one of the most respectable and trustworthy body of gentlemen in the country. Holding a distinguished position in

their respective localities, they are intelligent patrons
of industry and enterprise, and generally possessing
large resources, and conducting their affairs with
prudence and ability, they are perfectly safe for the
present limit of issue, and if any change whatever
is made in respect to them it should be in the direction of relaxing the present rigid limits. But on no
account should the spurious type of private banker
which was so common prior to 1826 be again
admitted into the ranks of the élite of the bankers
of England.

Proceeding next to the English Joint Stock Bank
issues, the limit of issue of the fifty-six issuers ranges
from 1,503*l.* up to 356,976*l.*, the average limit being
49,000*l.*, against a total paid-up capital of 8,000,000*l.*,
and an average of 143,000*l.* Here, again, there is
no ground for disturbance on the score of safety,
but there is legitimate cause for dissatisfaction both
amongst those within and those without the pale of
issue. A rearrangement should be made on the
basis of admitting on clear and uniform conditions
all banks carrying on business outside the radius of
sixty-five miles round London. The object to be
secured is equal-handed justice and safety, and the
latter can be attained in a variety of ways, the
most simple, and probably the most satisfactory of
which would be, to grant to all banks possessing a
certain minimum amount of paid-up capital, the
right to issue to the extent of a certain fixed proportion of the capital paid up. Too great a multiplicity

of issuers could be avoided by placing the minimum capital point sufficiently high for that purpose. Uniformity might be attained without injustice by confirming the present issuers in their rights for a period of twenty years, during which time the redistribution would be gradually effected, without injury to any of the interests concerned.

With respect to the Scotch issues, the present arrangement is most unsatisfactory. Whilst the six Irish issuing banks, with a capital of 5,730,000l., have an authorised limit of 6,354,494l., eleven Scotch banks have a limit of 2,759,271l. only against a capital of 9,400,000l. This anomaly arises out of the relatively greater material progress made by Scotland since the fixing of the limits thirty years ago. It is altogether indefensible, and when I remind the reader that it rests on that wonderfully erroneous theory respecting the foreign exchanges, I am sure the situation will be duly appreciated. On the grounds of justice and of common sense it is necessary that this absurdly low limit should be swept away; it is a landmark on the shores of error which cannot be too speedily attended to. The currency requirements of Scotland must be kept carefully in view on the one hand, and the general interests of the whole nation on the other. Under the present arrangement the law is a positive source of danger to the commercial interests of the whole country, a danger which in 1866 and in 1873 made itself tangibly felt. The remedy lies in the direction of throwing open the right to issue on the basis of capital, as already pointed out.

The Irish issues should be dealt with on the same just and uniform basis, due regard being given to the currency requirements of the country, and to the exceptional position of the Bank of Ireland.

With respect to the sixty-five miles radius round London, within which no bank, other than the Bank of England, is allowed to issue its own notes, it is in the abstract an anomaly, but practically it works to the advantage and convenience of the public, and should therefore be adhered to, with this modification, however, that those banks in London which have branches outside the radius, be placed on the same level as the Irish, Scotch, and Colonial banks, and be allowed, on the general conditions, to issue their own notes outside the radius. Some of the largest and safest banks in the kingdom are at present deprived of the right to issue simply because they have an office in London, and what makes the arrangement as intolerable as it is illogical and absurd, is the fact that this prohibition applies to the English banks only; the banks of Scotland, Ireland, Australia, and every other part of the empire being at perfect liberty to open as many offices in London as they choose, and retain their right to issue without running the risk of being ostracised in any way whatever.

These measures would considerably enlarge the present aggregate limit without necessarily causing the slightest addition to the actual volume of circulation—this point will come under notice in the next chapter, when I dispose of the question of over-issue —and the arrangement, whilst it would encourage the enlargement of banking capitals, and thereby give solidity to our financial system, would at the same time sweep away the rigid limits which were created in 1844 and 1845 for the purpose of placing into mechanical operation the erroneous principle of regulating the currency by the foreign exchanges.

With respect to the issue of one-pound notes, if any alteration is made it should certainly be in the direction of extending their issue to England in order to relieve the channels of circulation of the cumbrous mass of metal with which they are filled. Not only would the issue of small notes be a great boon in the saving in the wear and tear of gold, and the annual loss to the nation through abrasion, but a further considerable saving would thereby be effected in the heavy cost of the transmission of coin from place to place to which bankers are at present placed, and in the loss of that interest which would accrue if the gold was replaced by paper and invested. Those fluctuations in the central gold reserve which arise at various periods of the year, would also be reduced in extent, and a disturbing cause which has frequently operated injuriously be removed.

The State has an acknowledged right to a portion of the profits derivable from issues, and this can be secured by the continuation of the composition duty

M

which is at present levied. If any change whatever is made it should be in the direction of reducing the charge, particularly as regards the Bank of England, for anything like a hard bargain in such a matter inevitably recoils on the public in the objectionable form of a higher rate of discount.

It has frequently been proposed to make Bank of England notes legal tender throughout the United Kingdom. Many eminent authorities, both in Scotland and in Ireland, have advocated this step, and it is in every respect desirable. The principal advantage which would accrue from having a single central issuer, viz., the circulation of its notes in every portion of the kingdom, would be secured, and so long as the Bank does not issue notes of a lower denomination than 5*l*., it would interfere to a very slight extent only with the present privileges of the Scotch and Irish banks, whilst it would be a decided advantage to those banks by enabling them to keep a portion of their reserves in Bank of England notes.

If considered necessary, further security can be given to the note holder by the State enacting that notes shall constitute a legal preference on the assets of the issuers over all other creditors, and that in the case of limited liability banks the extent of liability on the unpaid-up capital shall at least equal the amount paid up. There are no end of financial devices by which any degree of security aimed at may be secured, and it will rest with the responsible minister to make a wise selection; but whatever degree of security is aimed at, due regard must be paid to the cardinal truth of monetary science, that narrow and rigid limits are fraught with danger, and must be carefully avoided.

The present arrangement is not only objectionable inasmuch as it is based on such a deplorably erroneous theory, but it has frequently constituted a powerful disturbing cause in the money market. This was conspicuously the case in 1866. On the 8th May the rate of discount was put up to 8 per cent. on a Tuesday, in the middle of the official week, a then very unusual course of proceeding. In my opinion, an opinion formed on careful observations made at the time, this step was a connecting link in the chain of events which led to that terrible panic. The public waited with bated breath to see the cause, assured that some very serious change in the position of the Bank had taken place, and the mere apprehension had a worse effect than a really adverse fact would have had, and as subsequent disclosures plainly showed, a steady run on a number of banks set in from that date. Now the only explanation ever given of this unfortunate rise was that 200,000*l.* in gold had been withdrawn for Scotland, and the Bank return up to 9th May showed that although the rate had been advanced from 6 to 8 per cent. within the week, the banking reserve had actually risen 175,000*l.*, whilst the total reduction in the bullion amounted only to 350,000*l.* It is deplorable to think that at a moment of such gravity so extreme a rise should have been made for so utterly inadequate and insignificant a cause. The real reason lay in the almost fierce determination of the directors that the restrictive principle of the Act of 1844 should never again be suspended. Smarting under the charges of a want of firmness, which had been openly preferred against them on previous occasions by Sir Robert Peel and Sir Charles Wood, and blindly believing in the perfect soundness of that utterly unsound principle, they acted up to the spirit of the Act with a vengeance, and would have deliberately wrecked the commercial prosperity of England if the City and the great centres of industry had not stepped forward and induced Her Majesty's Ministry to suspend the disastrous policy. And is it not a fact deserving of the most serious consideration of the country, that the directors are acting on this spirit up to the present moment, not maliciously, out of self-interest or in sheer levity, as many suppose, but in strict accordance with the expressed wishes of the Legislature? The responsibility of removing this standing source of danger to the industrial and mercantile interests of the country therefore devolves upon parliament.

CHAPTER IV.

OVER-ISSUES, SPECULATION, AND CONCLUSION.

THERE are two apparently powerful objections which are invariably advanced against all proposed measures, and which it will therefore be as well to at once dispose of. I allude to the terms *over-issue* and *speculation*. We will take that of over-issue first.

§ 1. Some people, and amongst them many who ought to know better, appear to think that the mere permission to issue notes free of any legislative restriction necessarily involves the actual issue of enormous quantities of notes, a reckless system of banking and credit, and tremendous speculation. They appear to dread it as an overwhelming source of evil, and don't hesitate to predict that universal ruin and destruction would inevitably follow such a measure. Now we have seen that the present system is based upon a similar idea, on the supposition that notes are a powerful lever for evil or for good; that by them, even under a convertible paper currency, the whole range of prices can be raised or depressed as the scientific manipulator determines, and that not only by increasing them can prices be raised, exportation of our products arrested, and every coin swept out of the channels of circulation and sent abroad, but that the currency actually is the sole and only cause of all exports of gold. It is true we have seen that this is a wild and utterly erroneous assumption, but the battle will nevertheless be transferred to this field unless we show that we are fully prepared to meet the foe. If you desire peace, be prepared for war. We will improve upon this maxim, and take quiet possession of the enemy's last intrenchment, and then give him his *coup de grace*.

A moment's reflection serves to dispel the fallacy. The expression *power to issue* has two distinct significations. 1. The *permission* to issue. 2. The power to place the notes into circulation and keep them there.

Now the power of banks to issue convertible notes, supposing no legal restriction to exist, is absolutely limited to the effective wants of the community. Within this limit they have the power to place them into circulation, and by the system of constantly reissuing them as fast as they are returned of keeping afloat the amount required by the community; but the extent to which they are retained in circulation is determined, not by the will of the issuers, but by the wants of the community. The will of the banker on the one hand and the wants of the community on the other, would under an unrestricted system mutually determine the amount in circulation. The extent to which banks exercise this limited power of placing notes into circulation depends again upon the nature and safety of the applications for discount and advances, the extent of their business, and the willingness of the public to take their notes in payment of cheques &c.; and the extent to which the public will retain notes and keep them in circulation depends upon the activity and extent of trade, and the degree to which notes are employed instead of coin and cheques. Then again the extent to which banks will extend their floating indebtedness in the form of notes depends upon the same causes, and the extent to which the public is willing to use credit and borrow money depends upon the state of trade and prices and the expectation of gain. It does not follow that credit will be given because it can be, or that it will be used because it can be obtained. The directors of banks have their own interests to consult, and it is absurd to suppose that they will knowingly make reckless and unsafe advances, and so long as they confine their operations to safe and legitimate business, no danger can arise from the issue of notes. The evil which arose from the issue of notes prior to 1826 was due entirely to that legislation which prohibited the formation of strong banks on the one hand and placed the issuing of notes in the hands of insecure parties on the other; the evil was an evil of credit, not of the quantity of circulation, and I have distinctly pointed out already, and now repeat, that the object to be aimed at is to place the issuing of notes in the hands of strong banks, possessing large paid-up capitals and sound credit. The advocates of the present system, with their usual ill fate, selected the wrong cause in this instance. They said the evil arose from the quantity of notes, whereas it really arose from the weakness of the issuers, and they attempted to uphold their selection by showing that the quantity actually increased to the extent of a few hundreds of thousands sterling; but unfortunately for their argument, Mr. Tooke and Mr. Newmarch met them on their own ground, and proved that the rise in prices which had been alleged as the effect of this insignificant increase in the issue of notes, preceded the increase, and was the cause and not the effect.

The error is the result of a confusion of ideas. Because the displacement of a gold currency by the sudden introduction of a paper currency on a large scale, would, by releasing the gold and throwing it into the market, disturb the equilibrium between the supply and the demand, and tend to lower its value, the error has been committed of supposing that every *fluctuation* in the quantity of currency after the grand operation had been effected, would also disturb the value of the whole currency. They overlooked the sound economic truth that if the fluctuations in the supply of any article exactly correspond with simultaneous fluctuations in the demand, its value remains undisturbed. The reason why the one operation would, if on a sufficiently large scale, lower the value of gold, would be because the supply suddenly exceeded the demand, but it will be observed these conditions are not present in the temporary fluctuations in a convertible currency ; for instead of the supply, the amount in circulation, exceeding the demand, it exactly corresponds with it. The substitution of the various forms of credit in the place of gold having once taken place, and the effect of the operation having been once produced, we may for all practical purposes consider their future effect as exclusively confined to preventing fluctuations in the demand for gold as currency leading to fluctuations in its value.   Credit is so elastic and capable of indefinite expansion, that every demand for an increase of currency is instantaneously met, and the tendency to disturb its value which the variations in the demand for currency have, is counteracted by a corresponding expansion of the supply.   Instead therefore of producing constant and violent fluctuations in the value of gold, as the advocates of the present system erroneously assume, the employment of the various forms of credit actually prevents many such fluctuations from taking place. The truth is exactly the reverse of the assumption on which the monetary system of this great country is based. The substitution having once been made we ought to aim at protecting the arrangement against any influences calculated to shake that confidence on which it rests. The substitution constitutes an important advance in civilisation, which cannot be carried to any considerable extent except under an advanced state of intelligence, just laws, and a sound and stable form of government.

As regards their effect upon the intrinsic value of gold, therefore, the mere fluctuation in the quantity of notes in circulation is immaterial, and instead of disturbing, positively imparts steadiness to it by instantaneously meeting the ever-varying demand. They have an effect, but it is diametrically different to that which has been attributed to them. It is because they are a superior form of credit, and constitute a part and parcel of our financial arrangements, that notes have so important a bearing upon the whole fabric of credit. So long as they are issued, as proposed, by safe issuers, and are convertible, it is not only altogether unnecessary to place artificial, rigid, and narrow limits upon their amount, but, as has been pointed out in the preceding pages, such limits, when they are too nearly approached, prove fatal to the safety of the whole fabric of credit.

The weakness of the fallacy is clearly perceived when we reflect on the fact that the purchasing power of notes is identically the same as that of all the other effective forms of credit, and exercises the same and only the same influence upon values. The purchasing power given by notes is precisely similar to that given by cheques drawn against deposits, discounts, and advances, and to that given by all the various forms of credit. WHETHER A PURCHASE IS EFFECTED BY A NOTE, CHEQUE, OPEN BOOK CREDIT, BILL OF EXCHANGE, COIN, OR IN ANY OTHER WAY, ITS INFLUENCE ON VALUES IS PRECISELY THE SAME ; AND IF IT WAS REALLY NECESSARY TO RESTRICT THE ONE, IT WOULD BE EQUALLY NECESSARY TO RESTRICT THE OTHERS. It is not, however, necessary to restrict any. Except in the case of a very large and sudden displacement of gold by the substitution of paper, without any corresponding demand for the gold, the intrinsic value of gold is not affected by fluctuations in the paper; on the contrary, it is rendered steady by such fluctuations. And values are not regulated by the quantity of notes, cheques, bills, or open credits afloat, but on the contrary, the amount of these is regulated by values and the extent and activity of trade. As we have already seen, values are regulated by the laws of supply and demand, and the instant credit in any of its various forms begins to produce effects which clash with those laws, it is at once counteracted. We may safely rely upon those laws protecting values against any tendency to disturbance which may be inherent to any of the forms of credit, and the folly of creating disasters in order to prevent notes revolutionising values is fully apparent when we bear in mind that the power of notes to do this is absolutely in-finitesimal. Under our financial arrangements, values float on a vast ocean of credit, banknotes con-stituting but a very small portion of the whole mass of credit employed. This is becoming more and more the case every day, as is indicated by the one fact, that the total of transactions settled through the London Clearing House, without the intervention of a single coin or banknote, increased from 4,018,464,000*l.*, in the year 1870–1, to the stupendous total of over 6,000,000,000*l.* in the year 1872–3. When we think of the enormous extent of credit which these figures indicate, it becomes clear that the molehill of a note has been converted by the unrestrained imaginative faculties of timid minds into a veritable mountain.

It follows from the foregoing truths, that it is not to the quantity of notes in circulation that the State has to direct its attention, but to the safety of the issuers. Provide a plurality of strong, safe, issuing bodies, but don't attempt by a system of leading-string legislation to dictate absolutely rigid boundaries to so important a constituent of our financial arrangements. Their power for good as a form of credit and as a medium of exchange is infinite, their power for evil infinitesimal. Bound up within narrow and rigid limits, they threaten the whole system with destruction, and the law has to be broken to prevent its breaking the Bank, and disorganising the vast industrial and commercial affairs of the country, nay, of the world, for you cannot ruin one State without inflicting serious injury on the cosmopolitan interests which are bound up in its prosperity.

It cannot be too carefully borne in mind, and I repeat it at the risk of being tedious, that banknotes are simply a medium of exchange, a form of credit, and a purchasing power in precisely the same respect as cheques are. Note issues, and deposits against which cheques are drawn, are equally liabilities on the part of the banker to the public, and the point to which the public has to direct its attention is in both cases the same, viz. the safety of the bank for its liabilities. It is to a certain extent incumbent upon the State to guard the public against loss on notes through the failure of the issuers, but it cannot be too clearly understood that this duty arises, not out of any mysterious or special influence of notes upon prices, for, as has been pointed out, no such special influence exists, but out of the fact that it is desirable that a certain degree of safety be secured to notes with a view to perfecting their efficiency as a medium of exchange. Cheques pass from hand to hand on the credit of the names which they bear. So do notes, but the credit is of a more general description, and it is highly desirable that a certain degree of safety be secured for them, so as to obviate the serious inconvenience which would otherwise exist. It is on this ground only that legislative interference is necessary. The faintest reflection will serve to dispel the transparent error of the supposition that there is any essential difference between a cheque drawn against a deposit, and a banknote issued against value received. In both cases the banker holds a consideration. It is true that the one is cancelled on payment, whereas the other is re-issued and made to serve in a series of transactions, but it is perfectly immaterial whether a given aggregate of transactions is settled by one piece of paper issued over and over again, or by a number of documents each of which is used once only. The point to be looked at is not the instrument but the values, the exchange and distribution of which the instrument merely facilitates. The laws of supply and demand will take care of the one, the proposed measures will provide every necessary security for the other.

Let us look at the matter for one moment from the banker's point of view. He regards deposits and notes alike as liabilities, and knows that if he attempts to push his credit too far he will be speedily called upon to provide the wherewithal to meet his extended engagements. If on the one hand he throws into circulation more notes than are required, the surplus at once rolls back upon him, and has to be paid. On the other hand, he has to provide against the fluctuating demand of his depositors, and restrict his advances on open account and discounts to within the limit of his means and credit. No doubt he may for a time succeed in extending his circulation of notes by availing himself of issuing them to parties likely to retain them for some time, or to place them into circulation to the exclusion or displacement of the issues of his neighbours, and no doubt he may, by re-discounting, enlarge his ability to make advances, but there is in both directions an absolute limit to his power of straining his credit, a limit too near an approach to which is fraught with danger to himself, and has frequently terminated in disaster. But although individual bankers may for a time succeed in doing this, the whole cannot possibly do it simultaneously. The public will not retain a larger amount of non-interest bearing notes than they require, and as the extension of the operations of any one banker is simply a diversion of a larger portion of the capital of the country into his own particular channel, it is evident that the aggregate of banking operations is not thereby increased.

What we have to provide against then, is not an over-issue in the sense in which that term has been generally understood, but against the issue of notes without such conditions as shall afford the public every reasonable guarantee against loss through the failure of the issuers. Prior to 1826 no steps whatever were taken to secure this desideratum, and the consequence was that the country was inundated, not with an enormous absolute quantity of notes, but with a quantity of notes issued by weak parties, who were the first to succumb to the storm. The banking arrangements constituted the weakest instead of the strongest point in our financial system, and their repeated breakdown lent a fictitious confirmation to the opinion that the evil lay in the amount of notes issued, whereas it really consisted

in the bad quality of the notes. It was a question
of credit, and if after what has been already said
any confirmation of this assertion were necessary, I
cannot conceive of anything more conclusive than
the following :—

It may justly excite astonishment that, notwithstanding
everyone who ever gave the least attention to the subject
must have been aware, that the bankruptcy and distress
which overspread the country in 1793, and in 1814, 1815,
and 1816, had been mainly occasioned by the defects
incident to the system of country banking, no steps were
taken in 1819, when the restriction on cash was set aside,
to have it remodelled and placed on a more solid foundation. Nations are slow and reluctant learners; and it
seems that additional experience was necessary to con-
vince the parliament and people of England that there
was anything defective in a system which in two previous
instances had deluged the country with bankruptcy ; *and
which enabled every individual, however poor or un-
principled, who chose to dub himself banker, to issue
notes to serve as currency in the ordinary transactions
of society !* The crisis that occurred in 1825–26 was the
natural result of this state of things, and might have been
anticipated by everyone acquainted either with the principles on which the business of banking ought to be conducted, or with its previous history in this country.—
J. R. M'Culloch's ' Wealth of Nations,' p. 499.

As this authority here admits, the weakness lay
in the defective banking arrangements. The principle of *laissez-faire* was pushed to extremes, and,
as Mr. M'Culloch points out, a man had only to dub
himself banker, and the most worthless of notes
could be thrown into the channels of circulation.

It was clearly a question of *insecure*, and not one of *over*-issues — a question of credit, and not of the mere amount of notes in circulation ; and the proposed measures will afford every reasonable security on that point.

I have had occasion to point out that Mr. M'Culloch fell into grievous errors on this subject, and was driven by the force of logical consistency into bolstering up the fundamental error—that respecting the causes of outflows of gold—by dressing up facts so as to lend to the whole theory an appearance of confirmation. But that unfortunate error of judgment does not vitiate all his opinions. He has done something towards building up the commercial prosperity of England, and, notwithstanding that he was misled by the state of public opinion and the confusion of ideas which existed on this subject, yet he is fairly entitled to a high position amongst the pioneers of progress, and to the gratitude of his country. In complicated subjects like this, and indeed in every branch of human affairs, the advance of truth is slow, it having to pass through a deep sea of error before reaching the surface. Even Mr. Mill, with his keen and powerful intellect, got entangled in this maze of error, and although his judgment asserted itself, and he condemned the system, yet he failed to detect the fundamental error on which it rests. Having adopted the ' ratio doctrine ' as an abstract truth, he was bound in its chains, and lent the great weight of his

N

authority to its support. He saw that it was logically correct. Grant the conditions or the premises, and it is the logical product; but as those conditions are the exact reverse of the existing state of things, have never yet been in practical operation, and are certainly far from likely to ever become so in the future, this abstract truth may be safely dismissed to the limbo of improbabilities, out of which it ought never to have been allowed to pass. It is much to be regretted that it was ever allowed to pollute the science of political economy, a science which, if anything, ought to be practical.

Before dismissing this point I may just call attention to the curious fallacy of confusion out of which the error appears to have arisen. The two propositions : 1. That the *quantity* of gold which would under an exclusively metallic currency be required as a medium of exchange would, if the metal was employed in every transaction, vary in an inverse ratio to its value ; 2. That the *value* of a convertible currency varies in an inverse ratio to its quantity,—have been treated as synonymous, whereas they are really distinct and entirely different propositions. The first is a truism which requires no demonstration to establish it ; the other is the very error which, as we have seen, is utterly untrue. The ratio doctrine is fully applicable to the first, being, in fact, nothing more or less than a form of expressing it, and the fallacy of confusion lies in its erroneous application to the second, a fallacy which is, perhaps, the most extravagant and glaring of its own particular species that has ever existed. The first proposition rests upon hypotheses not applicable to the present condition of things. Credit, instead of being entirely absent, is now actually employed in its various forms to conduct and complete transactions to an enormous extent without the intervention of a particle of gold. We have advanced, and left the purely metallic stage in the far distance. The proposition ceased to be applicable and became merely an abstract truth the moment our forefathers trusted in one another, the instant Time gave birth to Confidence, and it is a matter of moral certainty that this preceded the introduction of any medium of exchange whatever, and that therefore the hypothetical condition of things to which the proposition would have been alone applicable has really never existed ; and yet this is the very foundation-stone of the monetary system of this great commercial country at the present moment! Taking a very moderate view of the question, and accepting the generally received tradition respecting the age of our first appearance in this world, I am inclined to think that in practically acting as if the proposition was now applicable we are as near as possible some five thousand eight hundred and seventy-eight years behind the world in this matter. It is quite time we made a forced march and fell in with the front rank of progress. We are impeding the rate of advance, and causing the line of march to be strewn with wreck and disaster; in thus lagging behind we are guilty of a crime against humanity.

.   § 2. We will now proceed to examine a somewhat similar delusion, which is entertained by a large number of unreflecting people; and I will then bring these observations to a close, and launch them on the current of public opinion. The tide of truth is ever advancing, and errors are one by one being abandoned as we glide along the shores of time; and each one of us should, in our various paths in life, try to add our mite to the good work, the emancipation of the human race from weakness and from error. The time is rapidly approaching when sound finance will not simply be desirable, but will be of vital importance to this country—to the wonderful social fabric we are building up; and I venture to hope that long before that time arrives the fallacies which we have been examining will have been long abandoned and lost in the past.

Speculation is the other weapon with which every attack on these fallacies has been warded off. Overissue was the seed, speculation the tree, and disaster the fruit. The fruit we have found to belong to another tree, the tree of unsound legislation; the seed we have seen to resolve itself into a fallacy of confusion; and so speculation stands alone, ready for the axe of reason to cut it down.

Speculation, on examination, turns out not to be as black as it has been painted. It may be carried

to excess, and it has its weak side like every other
line of human action, but its weakness has been exaggerated and its value ignored. It is speculation
that regulates the distribution of commodities in
relation to the abundance or scarcity, and on occasions of great deficiency in the harvests, speculation
protects society from famine by raising prices in
anticipation of the scarcity, and in that manner, by
reducing the consumption at an early date, spreads
the deficiency over a comparatively long period. It
is true that speculation occasionally assumes an extravagant spirit, but this cannot be prevented by the
monetary system. The spirit was never so great as
it has been since 1844, and this simple fact renders
the objection futile. Low rates of interest have a
tendency to create a speculative feeling, but these
low rates cannot be prevented. They arise from the
abundance of capital, and unless we annihilated the
laws of supply and demand, which is impossible, low
rates cannot be prevented. Reckless or unfounded
speculations have a tendency to diminish as the laws
of value become more generally understood. They
also contain in themselves the principle of preven-
tion, in the losses which the recoil in prices inflicts
upon the holders. It is not the duty of a monetary
system to protect men from these losses; the only
safeguard consists in individual prudence, and if
knowledge does not succeed in inculcating this,
experience will. With our enormous commerce,
speculations are necessarily abundant; and as the

markets are so extensive, and such a number of
elements enter into the questions of supply and
demand, it cannot be a very great matter of surprise
if speculations should occasionally prove unfortunate.
Of course, after the event has taken place, there are
always plenty of people ready to cry out that it
was wild and reckless. It is difficult to define the
boundary line which divides legitimate enterprise
from speculation. Success is generally made the
test. The very same operation which, if successful,
will be applauded as far-seeing and praiseworthy
enterprise, will, if unsuccessful in its results, be
denounced as reckless speculation. The point, however, is that the present system does not prevent
speculation, and therefore this cry is no defence
whatever to the system based upon such deplorably
erroneous assumptions. For humanity's sake let us
be rational. If there is any particular form of
speculation which it is necessary to put a stop to,
take sensible means for its extermination. But don't
try to do it by the regulation of the currency by the
foreign exchanges; it would be just as rational to
regulate it by the phases of the moon at once, for
one is about as much calculated to do it as the other.
Take direct legislative action with respect to any
such particular speculation, as was done so successfully with that speculation in banking shares which
did so much to create the feeling of distrust which
preceded the panic of 1866. An effectual stop was
put to that by direct legislative action, and the same
course is still open.

One peculiarity about this cry of 'Wolf' is, that the very people who attribute every disaster to speculation after the crisis is over, are the very same people who came forward on the eve of the crash to assure us that, thanks to this wonderful Bank Act, nothing of the kind existed. Just prior to the crisis of 1866 it was declared that things were never in a more sound or legitimate condition, and yet no sooner had the disaster been inflicted than it was justified on the ground that it had cleared the commercial atmosphere of a speculative element with which it had been surcharged, regardless of the fact that this was no valid defence whatever to the system under which it was said to have arisen. Before the crisis the shield was declared to be perfectly white; after, to be black of the deepest dye. The fairest enterprise is denounced as the wildest speculation after the safest calculations have been defeated by a breakdown of the financial machinery brought about by the very system which these gentlemen stand up to defend, and if the falling off in our exports, which is at present taking place, without any corresponding falling off, but considerable increase in our imports, turns the balance of indebtedness against this country, and leads to an exportation of international currency—gold, it is assumed by our laws that this export of gold will have arisen from a redundancy in our currency, even although we may be in the enjoyment of a 10 per cent. rate of discount at the time ; and if it is suffi-

ciently heavy to lead to a crisis, through the operation of the law, many a house of fair reputation and
substantial means will be laid low, either through
the depreciation in produce, losses by the failure
of others, or inability to obtain the usual facilities
of credit; and the failures will, one and all, be
ascribed to reckless speculation and overtrading.
The absolute childishness of this cry was clearly
exposed by Mr. Baring in 1847.

During the debate on the Act, November 30, 1847,
Mr. T. Baring said, he was anxious that the debate should
not close without his having an opportunity of making a
few observations on what had fallen from the right
honourable gentleman, the Chancellor of the Exchequer,
with regard to that portion of the pressure which he had
attributed to commercial recklessness and overtrading—
that they could not rest the cause of that pressure entirely
on overtrading or want of capital. He would not deny
that there had been great errors, because he believed they
could not examine the affairs even of the most prosperous
and opulent houses without being able to put their fingers
on a number of blunders that they might have been
guilty of. If they were to look even into the Bank of
England, they might find it guilty of blunders; and
indeed the right honourable gentleman had that evening
charged the Bank of England with having overtraded
with government deposits (a laugh). He believed they
might even point to the Chancellor of the Exchequer
himself, and show that in the spring of the present year
he had overtraded with the credit of the country by
throwing a large number of exchequer-bills upon the
country, which there was not demand enough for to keep
from a most disgraceful rate of interest (hear, hear). The
right honourable gentleman had indeed committed several

blunders, which if committed by a small trader would
inevitably put him into the 'Gazette' (laughter). . . .
It was, he contended, a heavy charge for a leading
minister of the Crown to make, that all this pressure had
been produced by overtrading. He seemed to think that
it was only those who had failed that had suffered—that
it was merely those who had been overtrading who felt
the pressure; whereas the real fact was that the suffering
had been shared by the solvent portions of the community
just as much as by those who had overtraded. And what
the commercial body asked—not, as the right honourable
gentleman said, that they might be saved from their own
errors—was, that there might be means of preventing
those difficulties which the misfortunes of the country
brought upon them. What was the great complaint
among commercial men? It was that in certain circumstances, *by the present law*, it was impossible for the
Bank, whatever it might foresee in the course of trade, to
make advances upon the most undoubted securities, or to
continue its discounts. Surely that was not a satisfactory
state of things, and the commercial body had therefore a
right to complain.

Even Mr. Hankey, M.P., Director and formerly
Governor of the Bank of England, who is the last
of the defenders of this wonderful fortress of error,
declines to go this length in the direction of folly.
' *I am no advocate for any legislative enactments to
try and make the trading community more prudent.
I should be sorry to see any interference to prevent
persons overtrading or speculation. Let everyone
invest his money as he pleases; let everyone trade
on what capital he pleases, borrow money at what
rate and on what security he pleases.*'—(*Principles*

of Banking, p. 26.) Knowing from his own practical knowledge that the Act of 1844 does not in any way interfere with speculation, except in periods of stringency when it is quite unnecessary to do so, he does not even appear to have suspected that that was one of the declared objects of the Act which he comes forward to defend. Apparently overawed by the profound incomprehensibility of the reckless assumptions on which the Act is founded, Mr. Hankey makes no attempt whatever to support, defend, or prove them, but blindly endorses them as laid down by Col. Torrens, whom he quotes on the matter. *'The abstract subject,'* he writes, *'is one which has engaged the attention of so many able writers, that I should feel it to be presumptuous were I to attempt to throw fresh light upon it.'* He accordingly proceeds to argue in the vicious circle of which it constitutes the centre, and, as might have been anticipated, is compelled to commit himself to some very extraordinary, contradictory, and unfortunate statements. Had Mr. Hankey only brought his extensive experience of banking and finance to bear upon the transparent fallacies which we have been engaged in examining, he could not have failed to have detected the delusive nature of the foundation of the fabric to the defence of which he has lent the weight of his authority. But, as had so often been the case before, he allowed the enemy to all sound finance to pass on unchallenged, and so, unwittingly, became one of the defenders of one of the most extravagant fallacies that has ever deluded an intelligent people.

§ 3. It now only remains for me to point out the advantages which the proposed measures would produce, and I will then bring these observations to a close.

In the first place, commercial panics would be entirely prevented. By commercial panics, I mean phenomena similar to those which occurred in 1825, 1839, 1847, 1857, and 1866 ; the collapse of the credit system with all the attendant disasters. These were each produced by the restrictive system, and dispelled by its suspension and the application of the proposed system in a less perfect form and under less favourable circumstances. Fluctuations in the various branches of industry and commerce will never cease, but we shall cease to aggravate the difficulties when they do arise, and prevent their leading to a general breakdown of the whole of our financial arrangements.

In the second place, the rate of discount would be less fluctuating. There are two distinct classes of fluctuations : 1. Those which arise from the ordinary laws of supply and demand ; and 2. Those which are made by the Bank for the express purpose of checking drains. A drain of bullion creates a diminution in the floating loanable capital of the country, and a rise in the rate of discount is its legitimate effect. Rises of this class are generally

•

brought about by the open market advancing beyond the Bank minimum, and are generally of a moderate and gradual character. Rises of the second class are made by the Bank in advance of the open market, for the express purpose of operating on the foreign exchanges, and when exercised within reasonable limits this is sound policy in the cases of extreme drains. Under the present system, however, it is frequently carried beyond those limits. The Bank's bullion being divided, and the full brunt of the drains falling upon less than half of it, the effect on the Bank's position of a withdrawal of two or three millions is very much worse than it would otherwise be ; it produces a much greater reduction in the percentage of reserve to liabilities than it would otherwise do. The directors conceiving it to be advisable to correct drains at an early stage, put up the rate rapidly, as in 1866, and in the recent instance, and do not give it time to operate. They have adopted the policy of raising the rate point after point until the drain is arrested, and act on the rule that if a 5 or 6 per cent. rate does not instantaneously arrest the drain, to run up to 7, 8, 9, or 10 per cent., as the case may be. This has grown out of the restrictive system, and must be abandoned. As we have seen, drains arise from definite causes and are limited in extent. If a very heavy drain sets in, and it is considered advisable to check it, all that is necessary is simply to steadily maintain the rate slightly above the rates in those countries on the exchanges with which we wish to operate. By steadily maintaining our rate at from 5 to 6 per cent., and giving it time to produce its due effect, we can at any time calmly live out as great a drain as any which has ever yet arisen, or as is ever likely to arise. There is constantly a powerful flow of gold to this country from the gold-producing countries, and all that it is at any time necessary to do in order to reconstruct our central reserve whenever it has been reduced below the average point which it is considered desirable to aim at maintaining, is simply to maintain the rate of discount slightly above the mean rate. It is important to bear in mind that it takes a much higher rate to turn the exchanges and reverse the flow of gold than simply to arrest the flow. In the latter case a slight rise is sufficient to induce our foreign creditors and the exchange dealers to leave money here for employment, and give us time to fall back upon the constantly flowing bullion stream. A much greater rise is required to cover the expense of the transmission of bullion to us, and those extreme fluctuations and high rates of discount which the directors have adopted the system of making for the express purpose of turning the exchanges in our favour, will be altogether unnecessary. The wealth and resources of this country are so great, and the annual accumulation of capital is so considerable, that as the experience of the past completely demonstrates, there is no legitimate ground for fear that any temporary reduction of our floating capital will not be speedily made good out of our annual savings, and

such temporary reductions may therefore be calmly
endured without recourse being had to those high
rates and violent fluctuations in the rate of discount
which interfere so injuriously with mercantile operations. This fact, that it is not necessary to do more
than aim at producing an intermission in the export
of gold, is of the greatest importance. Its complete
recognition alone can secure the abandonment of the
present injurious policy.

It should also be borne in mind that it is
really seldom necessary that steps should be taken
to produce even an intermission, only when there
appears to be some very powerful disturbing cause
in operation which it is desirable should be counteracted. When an outflow is taking place to pay for
the additional purchase of food consequent upon the
misfortune of a deficient harvest, or in connection
with some national undertaking, such as a war, or
the relief of some distant part of the empire, in
such cases it should be the object of all to maintain
our productive powers in full activity, and the rate
of interest, instead of being arbitrarily raised, should
on the contrary be kept down as low as the operation of the laws of supply and demand will admit.
When, again, a foreign power has obtained a partial
and temporary command over our Money Market by
some causes over which, nationally, we have no
control, such as that obtained by Germany in 1872
and 1873, very great care should be taken that no
attempt is made to do the impossible. Germany
having determined to adopt a gold coinage, having

decided that the intention should be carried out at a certain rate, and having received from France bills upon this country, was able to command the gold, and could have taken it even if the Bank had raised its rate to 50 per cent. The rate did not in any way interfere with the operation. The engagements which led to the bills upon England had been entered upon months before, and no action of the Bank could prevent their being carried out. Every attempt made by the Bank to arrest the drain was futile, and it stopped only when the first part of the German programme had been completed. The rate may act as an inducement to delay, but it is powerless to act as a preventive to execution over engagements which have been entered into by the large and powerful firms engaged in these operations.

When gold is wanted to send abroad, they may make money as scarce as they like; it will go, because for what reason is it wanted? Gold is wanted if there is a war, and in that case foreign Governments will give 2 or 3 per cent. more or less for the gold, because they must have it. When the Emperor of Russia made war in Poland lately, gold which went from Hamburg to St. Petersburg and Warsaw was paying from 3 to 4 and 5 per cent. profit; if 5 per cent. will not buy it, 10 per cent. will be given.— *N. M. Rothschild's Evidence before Parliamentary Committee of* 1832.

And in the third place, the industrial and mercantile community will no longer be sacrificed to a rank fallacy. Those destructions or abstractions of our capital which arise from wars, deficient harvests, foreign loans, financial convulsions abroad, extraordinary absorptions of gold for foreign currency requirements, or any other of the powerful causes, will be effectually prevented from paralyzing our financial arrangements and inflicting misery, loss, and distress upon the country. Our central bullion reserve will be rendered useful and be made to act as a bulwark against general distrust, and our productive powers being maintained in full activity, it will be replenished without the infliction of the slightest injury on any of the great interests of the nation. An important advance will have been made in the application of pure economic science. Industry and commerce will rest on more secure foundations, and the further development of the international division of labour will proceed with a greater degree of safety. Based upon Experience, framed by Reason, and grounded in Truth, the monetary system of the financial centre of the world, instead of being a constant source of danger both to ourselves and to all commercially connected with us, will be a source of strength and safety to all the vast interests by which it is surrounded. Ever victorious in the past, when it has invariably rescued us out of the midst of wild disaster, it will be crowned with its well-won laurels, and serve the higher purpose of guarding and protecting us against any similar misfortunes in the future.

Spottiswoode & Co., Printers, New-street Square, London.

www.ingramcontent.com/pod-product-compliance
Lightning Source LLC
Chambersburg PA
CBHW030834270326
41928CB00007B/1054